DIY PUBLIC RELATIONS

Telling Your Story on a
Zero-Dollar Budget

Dan Shortridge

Fresno, California

DIY Public Relations: Telling Your Story on a Zero-Dollar Budget
© copyright 2022 Dan Shortridge

Published by Quill Driver Books
An imprint of Linden Publishing
2006 South Mary Street, Fresno, California 93721
(559) 233-6633 / (800) 345-4447
QuillDriverBooks.com

Quill Driver Books and Colophon are trademarks of
Linden Publishing, Inc.

ISBN: 978-1-610353-94-6
1 3 5 7 9 8 6 4 2

Linden Publishing titles may be purchased in quantity at special
discounts for educational, business, or promotional use. To inquire
about discount pricing, please refer to the contact information above.

For permission to use any portion of this book for academic purposes,
please contact the Copyright Clearance Center at www.copyright.com.

Printed in the United States of America
Library of Congress Cataloging-in-Publication data on file

Linden Publishing, Inc.
2006 S. Mary
Fresno, CA 93721
www.lindenpub.com

CONTENTS

Dedicated to Molly Murray,
a master storyteller who left us far too soon.

FOREWORD

Nearly two decades ago, I took a job in a newsroom where I had once worked as an editor. This time I was returning as a reporter. Talk about swallowing your pride.

It wasn't always an easy shift. I sometimes found myself working under people whom I'd trained, and the workload was always overwhelming.

One weekend night, I was the only reporter on duty and, as usual, my to-do list was longer than my arm. Between running out to accident scenes and checking police reports, I also had to follow up a story another reporter had left half-finished the day before about some union contract negotiations.

I managed to find a union rep at home, plugged in his side of the story, and shipped it over to the editor.

That editor, Dan Shortridge, approached my desk.

He asked if I had checked with the other side. No, I said. The other reporter did that before he left, so I did what I was supposed to. (I probably smarted off, too, something like "I had to move on to the ten other things I have to get to.")

There's a saying every old pro should know: "It ain't what you don't know that gets you into trouble. It's what you know for sure that just ain't so."

Dan saved me that night. We were going to run that story on the front page, and I would have had it 100 percent wrong. For the lack of one phone call—based on a misunderstanding, the simplest mistake that can be made in any communicator's business—we would have looked really foolish.

Dan never mentioned catching that error of mine to anyone, but it stays with me to this day. Your entire reputation can be at stake if you don't pay attention to the smallest of details because you're *sure* you know enough not to bother.

That wasn't the only time Dan shaped my work. He was a wonderful editor, always encouraging, always bringing smart advice, knowing exactly what will bring eyes to copy and pointing out exactly what is missing in a story that a reader will want to know.

So it was no surprise to me that reading his book, *DIY Public Relations: Telling Your Story on a Zero-Dollar Budget,* taught me even more about skillful communications, a topic I was pretty sure I knew very well.

Dan knows his job inside and out, communicates that beautifully, and has also consulted a number of accomplished professionals in their fields for their PR expertise. He breaks down real-life scenarios to show the reader step-by-step, comprehensive "how-to-put-this-into-practice" examples.

He shows what has worked for other businesses and, as a former journalist, he demystifies the process to get the attention of the media. This book is an invaluable and empowering guide for every organization, nonprofit, small business, or individual looking to raise their public profile.

The heart of good local public relations, as well as the heart of good journalism, is identifying and telling good stories. Focus on that, and you won't go wrong. Follow Dan's advice, and you'll find it easier than you ever imagined.

Rini Jeffers
Columnist, *The Chronicle-Telegram* and *The Medina Gazette,* Ohio
Two-time national award-winning columnist from the National Society of Newspaper Columnists
Multiple award-winning columnist from the Ohio Associated Press Media Editors, the Ohio Society of Professional Journalists, and the Press Club of Cleveland

INTRODUCTION

The news was not good: A particularly nasty tree-chomping beetle had been found in the next county over.

These electric-green creatures were tiny—about the size of a grain of rice—but incredibly hungry, going through ash trees like ninja turtles go through pizza.

I was in charge of public relations for the state of Delaware's agriculture department, and I knew we had to move fast to prevent people from worrying or panicking about this very real threat to their environment.

With just a few days' notice, we had to share the news with the public; get the word out to businesses that would be affected; preemptively address questions from worried homeowners about their trees; and coordinate everything with the relevant federal agency.

Most importantly, we had to do it all in a way that projected confidence and empathy, reassuring the public that everything was under control.

We quickly gathered our team together—scientists, foresters, and a small PR group—to come up with the right message and get it out quickly. We built a website, created a set of FAQs, strategized the most effective social media posts, and wrote a news release outlining the story we wanted to tell. And perhaps most critically, we gave the story in advance to a trusted reporter who agreed to hold it until the next day.

Early Tuesday morning, I pushed "send" and sent the news out into the world.

Everything worked. There was worry but no alarm. The reporter's story came out within minutes after our news release went out, with plenty of context and depth, and the rest of the media took their lead from her. Homeowners were happy to learn about simple steps they could take to defend against the beetles, and businesses like garden centers and nurseries were also pleased with the detailed communications.

We had taken potentially bad news and created a positive story, focusing on caution and prevention rather than worries and panic. We had answered the questions that people might ask with the information they needed to know. We gave local reporters and editors what they needed, too, including informative photos—and not inconsequently, we also strengthened our department's reputation as a trusted, reliable source for important news.

These kinds of outcomes are the gold standard in public relations. Of course, it doesn't always work out that way. But it's worth noting that we turned this story around with just a handful of people and a few days of hard work. We had no pricey PR firm on retainer, and we did it without buying a giant list of reporters' emails, paying to boost our social media posts, or subscribing to media-monitoring software. We managed the entire story ourselves with the resources we had on hand.

The same skill set I drew on here applies to much more than emergencies. Public relations campaigns celebrate good news as often—or hopefully, more so!—as they seek to mitigate bad news. The tips, templates, and case studies in this book will help you increase attendance at your events, share good news about new hires and promotions, get your mission and message out to the broadest audience possible, drive online engagement and social media shares—and yes, help battle potentially bad publicity about anything from company downsizings to ravenous green insects.

No matter what resources you have to call on, no matter how small your organization or your budget, you can always find a way to generate positive publicity and glowing media coverage. By following the lessons in this book, you'll learn how to tell your story the way it should be told, without hiring a public relations expert. In fact, by the time you've finished this book, *you'll* be the DIY PR expert, with all the tools you need to do it yourself.

— 1 —

PR ISN'T HARD

Public relations is the simple art of telling your story in the most authentic way possible. Like any specialized profession, PR can seem complicated to the novice, but it's really quite easy to master the basics and put them to work for you right away.

Forget what you may have heard or read about how hard it is to get good publicity. Don't pay attention to people who say that publicity has to be expensive. Forget about hiring a high-priced strategist or buying a secret database of contact information. Even if you have little or no experience, no staff on retainer, and not much of a budget, you can still succeed.

The simple fact is that as a small business owner, nonprofit director, school leader, local government official, or community group chairperson, you probably have a zero-dollar budget for marketing and PR. That doesn't matter. You can still get your message out to the press and the public professionally and effectively—all by yourself if need be. This book shows you how.

Any idiot can write a press release and post it all over social media. You can see the proof for yourself in the hundreds of useless, jargon-laden corporate publicity announcements posted online every day pushing new products, talking about improved packaging, or gushing over obscure business partnerships.

Few people will ever read those; even fewer will care. That's not how you want your story to end up. And it doesn't have to, once you understand what really matters.

You don't need to learn some top-secret trick or even turn yourself into a world-class schmoozing machine. What you *do* need is a deep knowledge of your organization, the ability to find and tell good stories, an attention to detail, and some basic human connection and awareness.

Tremendous Opportunity

Where I live, purchasing a half-page advertisement in one of my local newspapers would cost $440. Running a 30-second ad on the local TV station just once would cost hundreds of dollars at minimum—and that's for a time when few people would even be watching. During a prime-time show? Don't even ask.

By contrast, getting a half-page (or longer) story in the local weekly paper costs nothing. The same is true of a story in a much larger daily newspaper or a 30-second story on the local TV news. Zero dollars.

The bottom line: PR will give you the biggest bang for your buck every single time.

As a quick exercise, I opened up my town's daily newspaper one Saturday morning. In that single edition, there were 11 staff-written news items on a wide range of topics—local government actions, business profiles, and features on local neighborhood events. There were articles about nonprofit fundraisers, school open houses, new businesses opening, and much more.

Multiply those eleven spots by 52 weeks, and you have nearly 600 different chances every year to get your story out there—just in that one newspaper.

Every news outlet operates according to roughly the same considerations, especially on the local level. Television stations need local stories to fill up their half-hour newscasts. Radio stations want local sound bites to put on the air between talk shows. Online-only news sites require an endless supply of stories and photos to put something new and different in front of visitors and entice them into coming back for more.

Do I Really Need Publicity?

Whether you're running a small business, leading an organization, or managing a school, you have only so many hours in a day. You're getting pulled in all sorts of directions by many different priorities, and publicity may be far, far down on your list of priorities.

Here are some of the reasons it should be near the top:

VISIBILITY Media coverage can raise awareness of your mission, organization, or business. This is especially crucial if you're a quiet, behind-the-scenes type of operation, if your focus is mainly local or regional, or if your main issue doesn't attract a lot of attention on its own.

QUICK RESULTS A positive news story can have instant effects such as boosting web traffic, increasing donations, and growing sales.

GROWTH Good publicity in targeted media outlets can introduce you to new clients who wouldn't otherwise have learned of you or what you do.

AUTHORITY A properly placed story or column can help establish your position as an authority in your field—a "thought leader," in modern parlance. That helps give you and your organization expert status in the minds of readers. When they need help, they'll turn to you.

ONGOING ENGAGEMENT And then there's the downstream impact. In the Internet Age, news coverage has an almost unlimited life span online. Future customers or clients searching for your product or services or researching an issue you're passionate about will see that you have had consistent positive attention around that topic and aren't just a flash in the pan or fly-by-night operation.

Getting Started

I've been working in journalism and public relations for more than 20 years. In fact, I wrote my first press release in high school and got it published in the local newspaper without a word being changed. I had been elected our state's "youth governor" in a YMCA model legislature program, and with the ambition and self-confidence of youth, I decided that this was a newsworthy accomplishment. Rather than calling the local paper's lone reporter and asking him to interview me, I wrote something up and sent it in. It was just a few short paragraphs and a headline—but there I was on the front page of the paper a week or two later.

If I could do that at age 17, you can do it now.

Is It Really That Easy?

A successful public-relations campaign (or even a one-off piece) is not easy in the sense of being able to do it quickly. The details take precision, and the execution takes certain skills. You can't dash something off and expect it to work, notes brand marketer Justin Williams. Rather, he says, PR is "easy to execute poorly. Difficult to do well and break through the noise."

But PR *is* easy in that you don't need to have a professional PR firm on retainer to succeed. It is easy in that it primarily requires a willingness to look at things in the right way. And *that* takes creativity and a certain mindset. Above all, good PR requires awareness of your business or organization and the world in which you operate. Explains Kim

Hoey, a public relations strategist and freelance writer who's worked in both the political and nonprofit worlds, "I see opportunities and can easily see how they could be of interest to other people and which people would be interested."

You don't need to work for a marketing or PR agency to do this work well. Some of the best experts out there don't have degrees in PR or communications, and many were in other professions, such as journalism, before moving into telling peoples' stories for a living.

For years, Brian Selander has worked with the media, government leaders, and corporate executives in a variety of fields. He led strategic communications for one state governor and is now in the business world as a CEO himself. But he still keeps one thing in mind when working with the press: "It's not their job to tell *your* story. It's their job to tell *compelling* stories that maybe you can help provide."

Take a Good Look

To start from the ground up—to really look at your company or group as a journalist would—first take a few deep breaths and mentally disassociate from your organization. Forget the long hours, the hard work, and even the all-important mission. Move outside your body, take a few steps forward, and turn around.

What does this version of you see? What are your first impressions?

- Does your group's name and logo instantly convey your mission?
- Does your company's website have an easy-to-grasp explanation of the services you provide?
- Does your brochure have photos of satisfied clients and customers—or just boilerplate language and stock photos that could apply to anyone?
- What's the first link that pops up when someone searches for you online?
- When was the last time your Facebook page or Twitter account was updated?

- Does the last article written about you in your local newspaper get your primary objectives across? (If there even *is* a last article, that is.)

You're probably thinking, "What does our logo or our brochure have to do with getting a story featured on TV?"

The thing is, every impression point matters. If you claim to be an experienced marketing professional, but your flyers and brochures are illustrated with generic clip art, then your credibility instantly takes a dive. If your website's home page contains a misspelling or grammatical mistake, then it becomes ever harder to believe that your nonprofit pays close attention to other details. Your media reputation rests on all those other reputations. Local journalists live and work in their communities, and they're very much aware of the immediate world around them.

When I was a newspaper reporter, I always made a point of checking out the flyers posted on the community bulletin board at the grocery store and picking up brochures in building lobbies and visitors' centers to find possible feature stories. I read ads in the weekly newspaper to identify new businesses that might make good articles or future sources. I looked at business and neighborhood Facebook pages and groups to identify trends that my readers might be interested in.

The organizations that presented themselves professionally, put thought into it, and told a good story were the ones I was interested in talking with. The ones that didn't care about their presentation usually didn't get a call.

"It's fundamentally challenging," notes Ohio-based marketer Adam Horwitz, a former newspaper reporter. "Just like in marketing, your goal is not to only hit on the correct message, but also to keep the brand relevant throughout the year. Those are fundamentally difficult objectives."

No Special Skills Needed

Some of my colleagues in the industry may look aghast at me when they read this: You don't need a highly specialized expert-level skill set in order to do effective public relations.

You do need *certain* skills—reading, writing, situational awareness. But you certainly don't have to be a published writer or an award-winning photographer.

Many good public-relations people are former journalists. After all, virtually every journalist has been on the receiving end of a lot of PR—both good and bad. But as journalist and communications specialist Rachel Swick Mavity notes, a good PR person likely has a slightly larger skill set.

"While a journalist need only have skills to interview, write, and possibly photograph—a PR pro has to do all that and think strategically for the company," she says. "In addition, you likely also need web and social media skills, budgeting/finance skills, creativity (lots of it), a thick skin . . . and a strong go-get-'em attitude."

You also need curiosity, speed, flexibility, and endurance. Curiosity leads you to new and interesting information and angles; speed lets you produce material quickly and accurately; flexibility is the key to matching your story to the needs of each media outlet; and endurance keeps you going and maintaining your focus on the consistency we discussed earlier.

Do you have any of those talents? Then you're well on your way.

If you're strictly an expert in your own field without any of those other skills, then you need to learn them—by picking up a book like this, watching a how-to video, or taking a course. Your only other option is to hire someone who *does* have those skills.

It's Free—Sort Of

Of course, getting a story in the media isn't truly free—nothing is. There is a time cost—however long it takes to create and send out your story, at whatever rate you're paying yourself or an employee to do the work. And there's also the harder-to-quantify cost of creativity. Some people are just not natural writers, photographers, or schmoozers, and any job that requires those skills may be harder for them.

But those costs aren't primarily what you're looking at as a business owner, nonprofit executive, or government official. Rather, you're comparing the costs of doing this kind of public-relations work with the cost of running an advertisement in your local newspapers or on a local TV or radio station. You're comparing it with the cost of paying to promote a Facebook or Instagram or LinkedIn post. You're comparing it to the cost of billboards, yard signs, or any of the hundreds of other awareness-building tactics you could choose.

And compared to those, PR gives you by far the best return on investment. If it takes you two hours to write, edit, and send a press release about your nonprofit's new after-school tutoring program, and it gets picked up by a community weekly paper and your local TV station, that's a bargain compared to running an ad in both those outlets—and it'll be seen by far more people, as well.

If you hire a full-time staff person to handle your communications, or if you go big and put a PR firm on retainer, then yes, the cost will go up significantly. But most of the time, neither of those things is necessary for a smaller operation. Don't saddle yourself with the cost of an employee or a recurring contract until your PR needs have become more than you can handle on your own.

Types of Media

Before we dive into an entire book about working with the media, let's talk about "the media."

There are two different types of media: paid and earned.

> **PAID MEDIA** As you probably guessed, this refers to coverage that you pay for—advertising, billboards, and sponsored content. Reams could be written about how to manage paid media, and that's far beyond the scope of this book. Increasingly savvy

consumers tend to see advertising as inauthentic and sponsored content as the kind of scripted message that can't be trusted.

EARNED MEDIA This is the coverage that you *earn* based on your public-relations work and outreach. The message is seen as authentic because it hasn't been bought and paid for. Your story's worth has been judged and approved by an independent third party. (Local news outlets in particular are consistently rated as more trusted and more likely to report without bias than national ones.)

That's not to say that paid advertising doesn't have its place in the marketing mix. It can reinforce key messages, break through to reach new audiences, and be targeted very specifically to certain niche segments. It's just not the focus of this book.

Remember that public relations isn't the same as marketing or sales. Too many people lump all those terms together in one bucket. PR can work in tandem with a marketing campaign, and your PR efforts should be strategically planned to complement sales initiatives, but they aren't one and the same.

You'll learn more about the media and how it operates in Chapter 5.

The Importance of Trust

Working with the media is fundamentally dependent on trust, on all sides.

A reporter and their editor or producer have to trust that what you're saying is accurate and complete and that you're the person with the authority to say it. Building up that trust can take time—and so can rebuilding it, if you make a mistake. Establishing yourself as an authority on a topic—the go-to person for information about it—can take even more time, depending on the issue at hand.

For the general public, trust may take longer to establish. While most Americans place more trust in local news than they do in national media outlets, that still means only a 37 percent trust level, well behind local libraries (73 percent) and police (56 percent), according to research by Gallup and the Knight Foundation.

On an individual level, a reporter is only as good as the trust their audience places in them. If a particular writer or broadcast journalist frequently gives inaccurate or out-of-context information, or approaches the news from a particular point of view no matter what, then you may not want to trust them with your story.

If you're working with someone that you *do* have confidence in, it still takes a leap of faith to entrust them with your story—particularly if the issue is sensitive or highly personal. You absolutely must have confidence in the reporter's ability to handle the topic properly, respect the people involved, and be mindful of the broader impact a story may have once it lands in print, online, or on TV or radio. Above all, know that once you send your story out into the world, you lose control over it. Once a story is out there in the media, it's impossible to get it back. If you're telling a story for the first time, you've got one shot to get it right.

This is more than a little bit frightening the first time you're the one telling the story. Truth be told, I've been working in and around the media for two decades, and there are times I still find it nerve-racking to effectively bare my soul, my issue, or my business to someone I may have never met in person.

This book will show you how to build up that confidence and that trust by raising your knowledge of how the media works—and how you can prepare to tell your story to your maximum advantage.

Don't Be a One-Hit Wonder

When I was a newspaper reporter, there was one organization that I loved covering. Its events were photogenic, the news was genuinely newsworthy and could be tied into current trends, the narratives featured real people, and the leaders were always quotable and concise. I would have been happy to write about their work more often.

But this organization only made the news maybe twice a year, if that. The staff and volunteers just didn't make PR a priority—whether due to limited resources or a lack of knowledge, I don't know.

I covered a county of 1,200 square miles and 200,000 people and wrote about 300 stories a year. I didn't have a lot of time to check in with them more often just to ask, "Hey, what's up?"

As you go through the processes outlined in this book, you may realize that in fact you have only two truly newsworthy events a year, like the group I covered. But don't let that stop you from making news and getting better coverage throughout the year. You don't have to put something out once a week—you just have to be consistent.

When I started working for a local school district that had been battered by scandal, I made it my goal to put out a positive news item every two or three weeks. Often, our news would bunch up just based on the nature of the school calendar—for example, late August would bring a back-to-school story, a new-teacher story, and a new-programs story. But on average, we had a consistent calendar of news that kept the local weekly newspapers chock-full of positive stories about the district.

Think about the readers and viewers—the people you really want to reach with your key messages. Two stories a year aren't going to sink in and be remembered. That's just not enough frequency to change minds, attract customers, or get clients in your door.

But if your community group or school has an article, photo, or short news item in the weekly paper every other issue—just 26 items a year—those same readers will gradually come to know your larger story and to see you in a positive light. The volume of favorable coverage that you're getting will create an overwhelmingly positive impression in their minds.

Make Yourself a Resource

A consistent PR output doesn't just increase your coverage on a daily or weekly basis—it also keeps your name in front of reporters who may need a quotable source for a breaking news story or trend article. Does your nonprofit advocate for survivors of domestic violence? You'd be a great interview subject for any reporter looking into increasing reports of intimate partner violence. Did your musical instrument store offer virtual lessons for kids during the COVID lockdown? A reporter ought to be calling you for a story on how students sought out creative outlets even during a pandemic.

But they can't do that if they don't know you exist.

Try Again. And Again. And Again.

There's only one guarantee in public relations: You will fail.

That news conference you spent weeks planning will attract no reporters.

The interview you prepped your executive director for? It'll get cut from the newscast.

That perfect news release you wrote won't get published anywhere.

And the story you spent weeks working with a reporter on, giving them a tour, leading them to sources, and arranging photo opportunities, will get buried deep inside the paper where almost nobody will ever see it.

Any or all of those things will happen. Sometimes your story just doesn't get covered, whether because bigger news took precedence, a reporter got sick the day of your event, or an editor woke up on the wrong side of the bed and decided to kill the story. You can't let those failures discourage you. If you did everything that you could to get your story out, you just take the hit and get back out on the field. Start creating something for next time. Keep trying, iterating, and improving.

Consistency is your key to eventual success.

Start Small

It's all right to have big, ambitious dreams. Dreams are good—they keep us focused on the long term.

But when you're starting out on your public-relations plan, you need to start small and set yourself achievable goals. Going too big or too fast right out of the gate will leave you strung out and exhausted. Working toward smaller intermediate goals allows you to build your experience and your confidence—and achieving those goals will boost your reputation and profile.

Back when I was a newspaper reporter exploring alternatives to a journalism career, I had a job interview with a small consulting firm that wanted a PR person. Their service was important to a specific sector, but in a very behind-the-scenes way. They were not a household name, and their product took about five minutes to explain. I asked them what they would consider to be a success for someone in the job. "Getting us booked on the *Today* show," they answered. I cringed. Thankfully, I didn't get a callback for a second interview.

A national TV show booking is a great dream—but it shouldn't be your main goal or determinant of success when you're first starting out. Build up to that. You'll get there eventually—or somewhere equally as cool.

Getting Your Hands Dirty

My approach to public relations is simple: It's a job, not a lifestyle or a passion or a bunch of academic theories. PR is practical, hands-on, get-dirt-under-your-nails work. It's not the right field for people who want to gaze at the clouds and make deep pronouncements. If you spend all your time developing big-picture strategies and high-level concepts, you're a marketing director or creative chief, but you're not doing PR. Don't get me wrong—having a big-picture strategic view is very important. But you can't spend 100 percent of your day just working on strategy and still be good at the real-world work of PR.

The nonprofit communications director down the street who spent her day busting out two news releases, drafting a week of social media posts, talking with a local radio station about scheduling an interview, and fine-tuning arrangements for the media event next Tuesday? She's the one doing real PR.

Staying in the Background

I approach my work like this: I'm not being paid to get myself featured on the evening news. In fact, I consider it a failure if I'm the person quoted in a story that I pitch.

When I'm pushing out good news, my job is to give it a shove, stand back, and get out of the way. Positive publicity should highlight the leadership and staff of my organization. They're the ones who should be showcased and interviewed and profiled, not me. My role is to prepare them, pump them up, stand by if they need help, and then glide quietly into the background. That's a success.

The one exception is in a crisis. You'll learn more about crisis communication in Chapter 9, but my basic philosophy is that in those cases, it's my job to stand up and take the hits during an emergency or disaster. I'm there to take the slings and arrows.

The CEO or business owner or executive director or school principal may be standing up there next to me, but it's my primary job to play defense and protect the experts and staff so they can do their jobs. I'm the one with the tough skin who can just let things roll off my back. If I knowingly shove an unprepared and untrained staff member out in front of me during a crisis, I'm committing PR malpractice.

Measuring Impact

Your PR goals need to reflect your business or organizational objectives. The primary thing to remember is that if you don't track it, it doesn't exist—so invest a good amount of time in tracking your media reach and story results. If you want to raise community awareness of your organization, track placements in local media and connect that data to circulation or viewership numbers. If your goal is to increase web traffic, start by heavily promoting your website in your pitches and interviews. Then, turn to your website analytics and look for referral data. If your objective is to get local residents talking about an issue, then track mentions of that issue across social media, community forums, and letters to the editor.

Learning by Example

Throughout this book, you'll see small scenarios about imaginary people just like you in the fictional community of Smithville and how they solved their PR problems. At the end of most chapters, you'll also find a real-world story from someone who's been there and done that, as well as quotes, tips, and insights from successful PR people in a wide range of fields.

In the chapters that follow, you'll learn how to

- train and prepare to excel at interviews,
- organize a media event that gets your story covered,
- control your message in a crisis,
- research the right media outlet for your story,
- sort through the many important details,
- write a news release so it'll be picked up word-for-word,
- . . . and much more.

Let's go learn from the experts—and from people just like you who are in the trenches every day.

THE TAKEAWAY ——————————————————

Public relations work doesn't require any particular educational background or advanced degree, just a solid set of skills and an excellent story to tell. The story is more important than anything else, including connections with reporters and editors.

Here are the keys to building a great foundation for PR success:

- You will fail; understand that and accept it.
- Build two-way trust with reporters.
- Communicate consistent messages on a regular schedule.
- Understand how the media works.

- Start small with realistic goals and work your way up to the big leagues.

Remember that it's your job to tell your story. By doing that clearly and well, you can attract media attention and reach a much wider audience.

— 2 —

YOUR AUDIENCE

Smithville —————————————————————————————

Akari Tanaka's lifelong dream has been to open her own restaurant in downtown Smithville—and the dream is about to come true. Her new eatery is centered around dishes infused with maple syrup. The menu is tailored to customers who like natural sweeteners, but Akari knows that's a relatively small group to rely on for success. She has to think big—and broadly—to figure out who her other audiences are and how to reach them.

If you don't know who your audience is, you're doomed to fail. And the reverse is also true—understand your potential audience and how to reach them and you're likely to succeed. For example, the audience for an auto repair shop might be every compact-car driver in the county. A children's museum could target parents of kids ages 4 to 10. If your town's knitting guild is seeking new members, they'd want to identify an audience that loves to work with their hands. Before you do anything else, you need to estimate your audience's size, research their interests, and map out the best avenues for reaching them.

"My Audience Is Everyone"

Business consultants hear that a lot from aspiring entrepreneurs. In truth, your audience is *not* "everyone." There's no such thing as being for everyone. After all, even Walmart stores don't serve everyone—there are limits to the company's geographic reach. Not even Amazon aims to get *every* human on the planet to buy from it; some rural areas lack high-speed internet access. So if those giants don't target everyone, why would you be any different?

The fact is, every company, agency, or nonprofit serves a distinct audience. A charter school serves families, children, parents, and alumni. A carpet-cleaning business wants to reach adult homeowners who have carpets. A cookie-delivery service might cater to college students who want a late-night snack in their dorm rooms. And a hip apparel start-up could be aiming for an affluent high-school audience with lots of disposable cash.

Now you need to figure out *your* audience. That will help you focus and narrow your communications efforts so you're not wasting time and effort. Knowing your audience's characteristics—where they live, how old they are, what they do, how much money they make—helps you figure out where and how you can best reach them in their homes, on the road, in the larger community, and online.

Doing Research

America thrives on data. Companies vacuum up as many crumbs as possible about our lives—where we shop, what we eat, how far we commute, and what we wear. Those giant datasets allow megafirms—and smaller companies that can afford to buy data—to target us on an individual level through online cookies and other methods.

But good research on a target audience isn't solely the purview of big corporations with lots of money. There's a lot of publicly available data that you can dig up for free, with some careful internet research.

Let's begin with the US Census Bureau, which has a wealth of data on the people who live, work, and play in your area. Census data includes where people live, whether they own or rent, how old they are, their gender and race or ethnicity, how much they earn, how far their commute is, and more. Census data should always be your starting point for this kind of number crunching.

Here's how that can look in practice. Let's say you run a nonprofit organization that wants to provide services to veterans in northeast Ohio. Census data will tell you that, for example, in Wayne County there are more than 6,000 veterans, or 5.3 percent of the population. But neighboring Holmes County has just 1,500 veterans, or 3.5 percent of the population. You're going to get more bang for your buck in Wayne County.

The Census data will also tell you that in Wayne County, nearly 80 percent of households have broadband internet, while in Holmes it's only 56 percent. This indicates that you could do effective digital outreach on blogs and social media in Wayne County but should probably resort to print newspapers to reach your audience in Holmes County. (Holmes also happens to be home to a very large Amish community, which may be relevant to your data given that the Amish have traditionally not served in the military and hence would not be part of the audience for veterans' services.)

Local government agencies are another great source of data. Let's say, for example, that your local independent health-food store wants to reach more potential customers. From survey data at your county or state health department, you can find out how many adults eat five servings of fruit or vegetables each day. If that number is low in your area, then you can target that population with educational messaging and stories. Data on how many families with children live in the area as compared to single apartment-dwellers can help shape your messaging. You might want to focus on healthy lunchbox options over "vegetarian meals for one," for example, based on what you find.

Data as a Story Angle

Let's look at how this kind of data can also come in handy when you're developing good PR stories.

Imagine you're the owner of a kayak-rental shop that is expanding into selling camping gear as well. To figure out what gear to stock, you want to know how many people in your state go backpacking and whether day trips or longer camping vacations are more popular. Research from your state's parks department may give you those numbers, along with other data that can help you target people in certain geographic areas. Those figures can help you tell a good story to the media about how backpacking and hiking are a growing trend in your state or region.

For another example, imagine you're the head of a nonprofit organization trying to increase voter turnout. You can get a wealth of data on voting patterns from your local elections office, including party registration, overall turnout by election cycle, and turnout in specific races and by election districts. That data can be analyzed to create a story about how your nonprofit is fighting to reverse a decline in voter enthusiasm. The media will eat that up.

Don't forget that you can combine this kind of government data with publicly available private surveys to get a deeper perspective. Almost every business sector you can imagine has its industry trade groups, and many of them put out public reports on markets and trends. Your kayaking-and-camping-gear shop has easy access to national data showing that campers spend $1,500 on gear every year on average. From there, it's a matter of simple math to figure out how much money the campers in your area spend on gear each year. That's another good pitch point to convince the media to cover your business growth.

Gather Your Own Data

Don't forget that you are your own best source of information, says brand marketer Justin Williams. "Look to your own data," he suggests. "Customers, fans, followers, lookalike audiences"—all those represent the core base that you want to engage with, and you should already have much of that information at hand. You might just have to crunch it a little and ask some challenging questions.

To begin, dive into your website analytics and learn how to sort the data there; Google offers some great free Google Analytics training to show you how. Dig into your social media channels and look at past follower numbers and engagement—clicks, likes, shares, and comments. Look for trends: Do you get more website traffic and social engagement at certain times of the year? When you compare that to your business data over time, can you find a relationship between web traffic and sales? That trend data can help you with the timing of your biggest PR pushes.

Talk to Your Base

Now that you're armed with research and have data oozing out your ears, it's time to talk to your base. You can do that any way you like—a free online survey, a focus group, an informal chat with customers or clients. But you absolutely need to get input, feedback, and insight from your core audience. Ask them:

- What news sources do you read, watch, or listen to on a regular basis?
- How often do you read, watch, or listen to these sources?
- How do you consume them—in print, online, on TV, on radio, via podcast, on streaming video or YouTube?
- What other entertainment sources do you use—podcasts, television, streaming services?
- What local information sources do you read on a regular basis—"shopper" papers, blogs, community magazines, newsletters?
- What social media channels do you use on a regular basis, and what do you use them for?
- How often do you use social media, and what times of the day do you use it?

How do you get basic information about activities and events in the community, like concerts, farmers' markets, garage sales, community classes, youth programs, or competitions?

Finding answers to those questions will help you home in on where your audience is and how to reach them. You don't know unless you ask. You might find that a particular social media channel isn't widely used among your nonprofit's potential clients or that your school's parents prefer one local radio station over another. That is incredibly useful information that will help you make sure you're making the most of your PR efforts.

Beyond Free Data

If your focus is on consumer-oriented or business-to-business marketing, the landscape is a little different, and there are plenty of other books that will tell you all about that. For our purposes, free data and audience research should be sufficient to meet your most important need: understanding where and how to reach your base. But if, upon working all the angles detailed above, you find that you need more, be prepared to invest heavily. Software packages, consultant contractors, and in-house data experts can all help you gather the data you're lacking, but all those resources cost money. Often, a lot of money.

Still, sometimes it's worth it says Jeremy Tucker. His electric utility uses a survey company to help map out their key audiences. "This provides us with an accurate and broad understanding of how different segments of the public view our service attributes and our messaging," he says. "We create our messaging, ad campaigns, and media-relations strategies based on this data."

You may well be able to engineer a DIY alternative that meets your needs. I did just that when I worked at the Delaware State Housing Authority, which offers special loan programs for first-time and repeat homebuyers. We analyzed our own data on loans and combined that with population data, homeownership statistics, and website data, then extrapolated from that to create a customer funnel model that gave us a new perspective on our work and clients.

Smithville

IN ACTION: *To find out more about her base of potential customers who enjoy naturally sweetened treats, Akari Tanaka talked with nutrition experts at the local university. She also spoke with researchers at her county health department about the rise in obesity, diabetes, and other health conditions stemming from sugar consumption. She learned that her county and town have some of the highest diabetes rates in the state and picked up some public-health research on how to talk with medical patients about sugar. She put out a call on social media for people who wanted to eat healthier and sent respondents a quick survey about dining out to gather more information from prospective customers. That data and research provide the foundation for figuring out whom her messages need to reach and how she needs to start developing them.*

THE TAKEAWAY

Locating and studying your specific audience is Job One. "My audience is everyone" may sound inclusive, but aiming to reach everyone means an overly vague, too-broad message.

Data doesn't have to be expensive. Great free sources include the US Census Bureau, your state and local governments, private industry reports, and your own research. Do a deep dive into your website analytics and try talking directly to your customers and potential customers.

Sometimes it *does* make sense to pay for data, but wait to make that decision until you've seen what you can get for free. It's amazing how much good stuff is out there if you put in the time and effort to find it.

"What are we trying to accomplish?"

For a decade, Aaron Chusid led marketing and communications for the Boy Scouts of America (BSA) in the Washington, DC, region's National Capital Area Council. He got his start working for Scouting doing membership and fundraising. He then moved to a marketing agency working with the manufacturing industry before returning to the council.

"In that time, we've weathered some of the biggest stories to hit our organization, including [LGBTQ+] Scouts and leaders, to opening our traditional programs to female membership," he notes. "It's been a real education. Each year we learn something new about how to present ourselves to the public."

The DC council has about 60,000 youth members and 20,000 adult volunteers. In the Boy Scouts of America, it's the largest council in the country—"but in the grand scheme of things, we're a small nonprofit," Chusid explains. "Our summer camp brings in millions of dollars, but we also have to spend millions to run it. . . . So we have to be extremely targeted in what we're doing, and you really have to know going into it what you're trying to achieve."

That principle especially applies to understanding his audience. When he began leading marketing and communications for the council, he defined several key audiences: current members, potential members, parents, financial donors, alumni, and community members who are touched by or support the programs.

"There's no way to structure one campaign that will touch all of those groups," Chusid says. "So before we start, what I always push people to answer is, 'Who are we trying to reach? What are we trying to accomplish?' "

That approach worked well when the BSA opened up membership in its core, traditional programs to girls a few years ago. The program for 10- to 17-year-olds would no longer be known as the "Boy Scouts," but as "Scouts BSA." That required a few different approaches, says Chusid, including:

- a campaign to build awareness in the community about the change aimed at educating key audiences and dispelling myths and misconceptions
- a parallel campaign to educate current members, particularly adult volunteers, about the nuts and bolts of how the program would change—new training, summer-camp logistics, etc.
- a third campaign to recruit new Scouts, both female and male, who didn't yet know about the program and its opportunities

"While all that fell under the same umbrella, we had to approach it as three separate campaigns in terms of how we built the message and how we delivered it," Chusid says. "You couldn't take a press release written for the general public and then send it around to our Scout leaders and assume it would satisfy all of their needs."

— 3 —

YOUR STORY

Smithville

The Rev. Imani Thomas has been named the new pastor of Smithville Church. She's lived in Smithville for five years, working as a nonprofit organization's youth-program coordinator, so she knows a little about what the media likes and doesn't like. Her church's membership has been slowly declining for several years, and she wants to build it back up by telling a story about the church's vibrant community. She needs to figure out what that story is and how best to tell it.

A good story is something that touches the heart, inspires the soul, or engages the mind. It's a narrative that's new, exciting, and interesting, or one that provides some information or an experience that you can't get anywhere else.

Here's what a story isn't: anything that's boring, mundane, or routine. If your business is holding a sale, your nonprofit is recruiting volunteers to staff a booth, or your school district is paving a parking lot, that's not news. Those things are all run-of-the-mill routine activities.

Finally, your story shouldn't be too complicated. To be most effective, it should be distilled down to its most basic elements.

This chapter provides concrete examples of good stories by and for a local audience that you can adapt to your own circumstances.

What's an Angle?

The idea of taking an "angle" on a story sometimes gets a bad rap. Some people assume that it means a reporter or editor is approaching the story with a predetermined spin or bad intentions.

In reality, a story angle is just the perspective that a media outlet uses to tell that story—the specific aspect that it focuses on. An angle can link to a particular trend, address a special challenge, or give additional value to readers. Over the long term, you can tell a story about a general topic many different ways, using a new angle each time.

What makes a good hook or angle for a story that you're pitching to the media? Here are some of the most common story types used by the press to tell stories and PR people to pitch them:

> **FIRSTS** The first of something is almost always going to get attention from the press. Are you the first health care clinic in your area to offer bilingual health services? Is your school's graduating class the first to finish with all A's or B's? Is your web-design business the first in your county to use new ADA-compliant design standards for people with disabilities? Are your tree-care firm's new arborists the first in the region to have earned some new certification or credential? Being first in a substantive category is an excellent news angle. Just keep in mind that the narrower and more specific the category, the less general interest there will be. The first woman-owned home-construction company in your area may get some good press; the first millennial-owned home-construction company led by a female graduate of Georgia Tech probably won't get attention, outside of a small circle of alumni.
>
> **STARTS AND FINISHES** A business opening its doors, a nonprofit launching a program, or a school beginning the year—those are all obvious examples of openings, signifying a new start, approach, or initiative. Just being new doesn't make it news, of course; you have to make sure your story is important,

has value to other people, and is placed in an interesting context. But a new venture usually does make it into the news category. Over the past year I've noted stories about a university offering take-home COVID-19 tests to students, a city government starting pickup of curbside compost, and a preschool launching a "Grandfriends" program to bring children and older adults together. A story could be written about each of those initiatives at any stage, but the first news hook is naturally at the start.

What about endings? You may not think of something wrapping up as being a positive story, but it all depends on the details. For example, a nonprofit may end a hunger-fighting project because the need for its services has declined significantly in the area. The media will certainly be interested in such stories and will seek them out whether or not you want that story told—so always be thinking about how to frame it in a positive way.

MONEY As the song goes, money talks. Big amounts of money, or even small amounts of money that will affect a lot of people, are almost always interesting to the media. Did your nonprofit sign a major contract? Did your school board reduce property-tax rates? Did your business increase its minimum wage significantly? When I worked in state government for our agricultural agency, I became closely attuned to the fluctuations in funding for the state's farmland preservation program, which was a subject of interest every year in the press.

Similarly, reductions or increases in government budgets can affect the private sector—for example, increases in child-care assistance can be shown to have a positive impact on early childhood education programs. A smart preschool owner could present that information as a news hook to get the media to write about how state funding is making a new immersive Spanish-language program possible.

DONATIONS In the world of nonprofit organizations, a significant donation can be a big story. Depending on your group's size, thousands or hundreds of thousands of dollars may be worth talking about. You can always frame a small amount of money as a percentage of your organization's budget to create an impressive story. A $5,000 donation might not be much to a large foundation, but to a community organization with a $50,000 budget, that's 10 percent of the money they would normally need to raise.

Trends over time, not just snapshots of single gifts, are also newsworthy. If your donations have increased 22 percent over the last five years, that's big. If your base of small-dollar donations has gone up significantly, that's also a good story that can showcase the community's love for your cause.

The identity of an individual donor may also make for a bigger story. My local historically Black university, Delaware State University, recently received a $20 million gift. That would have been huge on its own, but the fact that it came from philanthropist MacKenzie Scott—the former spouse of Amazon founder Jeff Bezos—made it part of a national story and got the donation even more prominent treatment locally. Some donors, of course, want to be anonymous; that can create a bonus for getting media interest, as it adds a hint of mystery to the story.

CURRENT AFFAIRS Piggybacking off a topic in the national or international news can also get you good coverage—but only if you're one of the first to make the connection. When COVID-19 erupted here in the United States, the school district I worked for at the time quickly assembled medical supplies, including gloves, hand sanitizer, masks, gowns, and other personal protective equipment to donate to local hospitals. Our school nurses raided their cabinets for anything they could spare, and our vo-tech high school's nursing career program contributed extra supplies. Our news release got widespread media attention and led to increased donations and public support for local hospitals during a time when they were experiencing shortages of basic supplies. If we'd put out a story a week or two later, someone else would have been first and our announcement would have been ignored.

RESEARCH If your organization's data can shed light on a local or regional situation, circumstance, or problem, then you can highlight that to draw attention to solutions—and ultimately benefit your cause. If you don't have the resources to conduct an in-depth statistical analysis, or if you think the public may not trust the information if it comes directly from you, explore a partnership with a local college, university, or foundation that has expertise in this area. That validation by a third party can lend tremendous support to getting your issue covered. For example, when the University of Pennsylvania's medical school did research into the impacts of a Philadelphia home-assistance program, it got media attention as far afield as Denver.

GEOGRAPHIC EXPANSION Most local media outlets just focus on their local area, whether that's a city, a county, or a general region. But there are always larger newspapers and television stations up the food chain looking for bigger trends and stories that cross multiple local areas. If your Southern BBQ food-truck business is expanding from Lexington to Louisville, Kentucky, because so many people are willing to drive over an hour just to get your grub, that's a great story. If your mental-health non-profit is growing to cover a new county that has lacked crucial counseling and psychiatric services, that's a story the media will want to tell.

DAVID VS. GOLIATH Everyone likes a tale about a little guy—a very little guy—triumphing against all odds against a much larger, more experienced, and better-equipped opponent. The media adores scrappy-little-upstart stories, even more so when that upstart is facing off against a giant. That applies to anything—a family-owned hardware store challenging a large corporate chain, an antismoking nonprofit going up against the vaping industry, a specialty food shop taking on a megastore.

ANNIVERSARIES It's odd to think how a simple turn of the calendar can create a great news hook, but it's true. The anniversary of a historical event, program launch, or business's founding can be a good draw for getting the media interested. Law enforcement agencies rely on anniversaries as a useful tool for bringing new attention to unsolved cases. A big-ticket anniversary—say the 50th or 100th—can provide an opportunity to explore the history of your cause or organization. A more recent time period—a 5th or 10th anniversary—gives you the ability to reconnect with recent alumni or former team members. Go for a nice number ending with a 0 or 5.

NATIONAL CELEBRATION Almost every cause, industry, or group has some sort of day, week, or month commemorating its accomplishments, history, or passions. There's National Salami Day in September, American Craft Beer Week in May, and National Mentoring Month in January. A simple web search can identify multiple options for your organization to celebrate. Connect the calendar item with a special event, statistical update, or local celebration to upgrade your news hook. Your industry trade group may be able to provide background information about the occasion. One great thing about using an annual celebration to attract news attention is that you have plenty of advance notice to prepare; if you missed it this year, you can always get ready for next year.

BREAKING A RECORD If you have an especially creative team, or if you're an organization that caters to youth, you may have a cool opportunity for some one-off press attention—by setting a new record. Whether we're talking about a world record from the Guinness book folks or a local or state record, the media loves these stories. One great example I've seen was a nonprofit organization that honors Purple Heart recipients making news when they received donations raised by a Marine veteran who set a record for the most push-ups in a single hour. It is worth noting that the Guinness records in particular can get very stunt-like—largest dinosaur flash mob, anyone?—so make sure the record is related to your greater purpose or mission for maximum impact.

COMMUNITY SERVICE For local businesses, showing your dedication to your community is both a good cause and a good opportunity for publicity. Make a monetary donation, give an in-kind gift of goods or services, or pay your employees for a day of volunteering each month. A construction company in my area got a huge burst of attention when it led an "Extreme Home Makeover" effort to benefit a local soup kitchen. Those items can build significant goodwill in the community.

SEASONAL TRENDS Some stories naturally go along with certain times of the year. There's back-to-school season, Thanksgiving, winter clothing purchases, the winter holidays, and more. If your school, nonprofit, or business can develop stories that link to those seasonal milestones, then you will have an extra hook in making your pitch.

NEW TECHNOLOGY In an age of overnight technological change, being the first to adopt new tech isn't quite the major angle it once was. But new technology can still be part of a good story if handled correctly and placed in the right context. For example, the school district I worked for became the first in our county to use a mobile app that connected staff and faculty instantly with 911 dispatchers, including texting capabilities—a great tool during an active emergency. That got us some strong news coverage and also served as a main messaging point with the community on school safety and security.

A Classic Angle

One of the most basic and satisfying types of story is that of "person vs. thing," or overcoming conflict. To frame this for your messaging, ask yourself who or what are you fighting against. It's all a matter of perspective—looked at the right way, even a fabric store or after-school kids' program has an opponent.

- The fire company fights fires, sure—but also risk, destruction, chaos, pain, and loss.
- The local hardware store helps homeowners, renters, and business owners battle Murphy's Law—what can go wrong, will, but with the right tools you can prevail.
- The martial arts studio is fighting against a lack of discipline and focus.
- The city council candidate is fighting against gentrification, crime, and traffic—but also against other candidates, which allows them to personify the problems and challenges they're battling.
- The produce farmer is fighting against prefab TV dinners, fast-food takeout, and packaged snacks.
- The get-out-the-vote nonprofit is fighting against sloth and a lack of interest in our democracy.
- Oh, and the fabric store? It's fighting against the erosion of our nation's once robust DIY mindset and our addiction to screens.

Give yourself an opponent to fight. Even if you don't talk about *fighting* directly, that approach can still inform and help your messaging.

Smithville ───────────────────────────────

IN ACTION: After talking with many of her church's members, Rev. Imani Thomas has identified several stories that she wants to pitch to the media. The main story is about how her church's membership has become more diverse, with more LGBTQ+ families and people of color joining, as well as a recent increase in young families with small children. One angle focuses on the church's upcoming special service for Pride Month, which would also be a chance to showcase its childcare service for little kids. She has decided to invite the local newspaper's features reporter and a TV reporter who specializes in diversity and equity to give them both a behind-the-scenes look and a talk with her members.

A New Solution to an Old Problem

The media loves to uncover new ways of fixing problems. Innovation and solutions can be key elements of a good news story, especially as many media outlets have pivoted to what's called "solutions journalism"—investigating and highlighting successes rather than just focusing on problems.

One example: For years, public schools have suffered from a shortage of qualified substitute teachers. Low pay, high stress, and an aging pool of retired teachers have all contributed to severe problems with recruiting and retaining on-call staff. In 2019, the school system I worked for tried to solve the issue by creating a set of permanent substitute positions—subs who would be guaranteed a minimum number of hours each week. The idea was to provide consistency to these valuable team members. Our announcement of that initiative got coverage in several local papers and provided one TV station with a hook for a story about the shortage locally.

During the early months of the COVID-19 pandemic, many groups and agencies had to adapt to new ways of operating just to provide basic services, products, or programs. One such case is a

Philadelphia-based regional nonprofit called Mighty Writers, which offers after-school writing workshops and evening classes for kids and teenagers. Unable to bring the kids together in person, it created a new venture that distributed food boxes to participating families—along with young-adult novels, children's books, and bilingual writing worksheets. It was a way to reach families who were underserved by local food distribution sites while continuing to engage the youth with writing and school support. The effort got strong positive articles in the *Philadelphia Tribune,* a newspaper dedicated to Black issues, as well as a sustainability magazine, a local social-impact blog, and a regional public television station.

Doing Usual Things in an Unusual Way

Making beer isn't particularly newsworthy, even though the craft beer explosion of recent years has led to countless new local breweries producing some great products. A new brewery opening up may lead to a headline or two at the launch, but how do you keep that interest going and spark new stories?

Sam and Mariah Calagione, founders of Dogfish Head Brewery, are masters at getting press for the company's "off-centered" beverages. Their team once created an ale called Pangea, named for the single original continent on Earth, which incorporated ingredients from every continent today, including basmati rice from Asia, maize from North America, and water from Antarctica. Another limited-run beer, called Celest-jewel-ale, was made with crushed meteorites. Dogfish Head then worked with a local company that manufactures space suits to create koozies out of space-suit material. The unique mix of ingredients led to numerous stories about the weird beers being brewed in Delaware, building Dogfish's reputation around the country.

Catching the Trend Wave

Journalist Rachel Swick Mavity reminds us that trends are key to pitching your story. Many reporters won't write about one specific project, but they will be eager to jump on something that can be quantified as increasing or decreasing somehow. That's news. At a hospital she formerly worked for, the process went like this:

> The public-relations team monitored and tracked news stories about particular topics, identifying when there was a cluster of items around a specific issue.
>
> Then, the staff checked into whether the hospital had an expert who could talk knowledgeably about that topic.
>
> Once an expert was identified, a PR writer worked up an "abstract of information" from that expert, including context that "helps the reporter see the whole story" and quotes that might end up in the final article.
>
> Finally, the team pitched the story and the expert to the publications they thought would be the best fit, from local to national outlets.

"In some cases, the information we pitch will end up being part of a larger story, but it all helps get your name out there," she says.

An example of this kind of process might be sourcing an expert perspective on how to prevent injuries at the beach—scrapes from the sand, head injuries from the surf, jellyfish stings, sunburn, etc.—pitched to media outlets that cover popular summer coastal areas and tourist destinations.

Feature Stories

When you're identifying potential stories inside your organization or business, there will be some that instantly strike you as being "news." These are fresh, flashy, new—the type of stories you see kicking off your local news broadcast or read on the front page of the newspaper.

But what about those stories in the middle of the newscast or in the inside pages of the paper? Where do they come from?

They aren't just lower-level or less important news stories. In the news business, they're called features—stories that report on a trend, analyze a cultural issue, profile a person, or showcase an interesting or entertaining topic. They can illuminate an important issue, draw attention to a cause or problem, or highlight an underreported aspect of a situation.

The "features section" in many newspapers may still carry the stigma of being "softer" coverage about food, fashion, home, or gossip. Back in the day, these stories were often placed on the so-called women's pages. But today, some of the best feature writing in the United States is about serious, hard news topics. Recent Pulitzer Prize–winning feature writers have tackled global migration, the war on terror, and the hunt for mass murderers.

What differentiates these stories from their hard-news counterparts is not the subject matter so much as the approach taken by the reporters. These pieces set out to explore or explain a topic, rather than hitting the reader over the head with a just-the-facts style. Where news stories jam the who, what, when, where, why, and how into a few short paragraphs, a feature story offers analysis and context, emphasizing the importance of the topic at hand. Instead of a straightforward, direct news lead, feature stories often begin with a story-within-a-story—what we call an "anecdotal lead," a short vignette that cuts to the heart of the issue.

Some of the best stories I've been able to tell in the news have been feature pieces. During the first year of the pandemic, my vocational-technical school district wasn't able to bring any reporters onto the campus. One of the ways I told our story was through a feature on a program that sent seniors into the workforce to gain real-world, hands-on career experience. I gathered information from a handful of high-school seniors who were working in the middle of COVID-19, got a few photos, and wrote a story that led with a young woman in our electrical program who had been at work wiring homes, replacing breakers, and updating bad receptacles.

There was nothing particularly newsy about the story; if I'd tried to write a traditional news lead, it would have fizzled. But leading with the student's story, emphasizing that it was part of a trend, focusing on the fact that students were continuing to learn these skills during COVID-19, and showcasing statistics about the program's growth all came together to make for an excellent article that got published across our local market.

People in Business

Your local newspaper or regional business publication probably has a regular feature titled "People in Business," "People on the Move," or something similar. This is a great place to get good publicity for your new employees or board members. Write a short paragraph about each one, including their professional background and what brought them to your organization, and submit it with a good-quality photograph. Most publications run these items verbatim with very little editing, so write crisply and clearly. Your business or organization's prospective clients will be reminded that you're out there, you'll benefit from the focus on the expertise and authority your hires bring, and your new team members will enjoy the attention. Law firms, accountants, and other professional services firms frequently do a great job of this.

Petitions

Petitions can be an easy way to get attention for a cause, especially if you are working with an issue- or mission-based organization. A petition can demonstrate public support or opposition to your core issue and is an easy way for the media to gauge local interest. However, there are multiple pitfalls you must avoid.

First, you need to ensure that your petitions are rock-solid. Faked signatures or made-up names will scuttle your effort before it begins. There have been multiple political candidates whose campaigns have fallen short when a petition to get on the ballot was faked. Especially if you're working with a paid signature-gathering consultant, do your due diligence to make sure your data is impeccable. If this is a high-profile issue, reporters are at least going to do a cursory spot check, so you should too.

Second, the more prominent your issue or the larger your area, the more signatures you need to have. A couple hundred signatures about an issue affecting a single neighborhood will be of greater consequence than a thousand signatures for an issue affecting a much larger congressional district. You'll need more signatures on a petition about the public schools than on one about municipal tennis courts.

And third, media outlets have come to regard online petitions with increasing skepticism. There's no way to verify that all the signers are from your area; an especially popular petition on an online petition-gathering platform can get signatures from people all over the country or world. Having 5,000 signatures sounds impressive, but the local media likely won't care unless they're from your local residents.

Always Room for Improvement

Don't settle on the first idea for a story that comes into your head. There are always ways to improve on an idea. Let's look at two examples.

You are the operations manager for a veterinarian's office that's looking to get some media attention. Someone suggests offering a limited-time discount of 10 percent off all services. That's an advertisement; no news outlet is going to cover that. Another staff member proposes holding a free spay-and-neuter drive for newly adopted pets. That's a story. What if you hold the free clinic and also offer additional services at a discount to low-income pet owners? That's a *good* story.

You are the new PR manager for a school trying to attract more attention from local parents. The superintendent wants to hold an open house—but as you know, that's a calendar item, not a full story. The science department chair proposes holding a free science day with activities for all ages. That's a story. The facilities director wants to hold the science event and also use it to promote the school's investments in the environment—a solar field, low-flush toilets, reusable water bottles, and community rain barrels. That's a *great* story.

Going Deep

A story has to be more than just an angle. If all you have is an angle, without any depth or details, the media will pick up on that instantly— or your story will deflate in the middle of an interview once a reporter asks some probing questions. Your story must be complete with characters, supporting data, context, impact, history, and value. The first angle you select may not be the right one or may not lead to a complete story. Keep on working at it until you get there.

But don't delete your imperfect angles! A pithy introductory paragraph or quippy line may not be enough for a story—but it can be turned into a solid social media post. You don't need as much raw material for that type of content. See Chapter 10 for a more detailed explanation and examples.

Evergreens

So-called evergreen stories are equally fresh at any time of the year. They can run at virtually any time without losing their impact or value and can be banked to reuse as needed. Your hardware store can offer advice on repairing flood damage. A youth-serving nonprofit can give parents tips on helping with homework. And an independent school can provide information on how to ace college applications.

Evergreen stories are often used as filler inside newspapers on a slow day or week. You should write them in a standard news style (see Chapter 4), putting the most important information at the top in case the story needs to be cut for space.

To identify a good evergreen story, start with the questions that your business or organization gets asked most often—not about you but about the problems that you help people solve. Work on items that showcase your expertise and bring real value to the reader. Not everyone is going to be interested in those topics, of course, but those people who are will be captured by your headline and consider you an authority.

Publicity for a Person

Most of our discussion so far has focused on getting media attention for an entity or a cause—a nonprofit, a business, a school, or a government agency. But what if you're trying to get coverage for a specific person? As strange as it might sound, there are some standard differences that you need to consider and plan for.

Let's review some examples first, because this concept can be difficult to grasp as an abstract.

If you're working on a local political campaign, then your cause is your candidate. You don't have a larger organization that you're working on behalf of—your mission is to get positive publicity for one person and their associated issues.

You might also be doing PR for a consultant whose business is tightly linked to their name. In many consulting fields, the work is highly personal and built on one-to-one relationships, so consultants often use their identity as their business brand.

Or you could be working with a solo business where the core work is done by one person, such as a doctor, a graphic designer, or a personal trainer. These businesses might have support staff—a nurse or office manager, for example—but they wouldn't be there without that person they're supporting.

Here are some key considerations for this type of a business or organization:

GET THE VOICE RIGHT Become very familiar with the person's voice and tone before you start putting together quotes or writing talking points. Make sure you're writing how they talk naturally, especially if they have a very distinctive style or if speaking is a major part of their business (think a professional public speaker or a politician).

GET SIGN-OFF Ensure that all material that goes out to the press gets a review by the person involved. In a larger nonprofit organization, the CEO might not have time to look over every single media advisory and tip sheet and may delegate that to another senior staffer. But in this instance, where their personal branding is their livelihood, you need to make certain they have eyes on all of it.

GET PERSONAL When doing social media or op-eds, write from an "I" perspective. For an organization or larger business, you often write from the organizational viewpoint and use "we" a lot—but there is no "we" when writing for a one-woman consulting firm.

BUILD THE RIGHT BIO Work closely with the person to build their biography statement. This is a tightly written paragraph that gets featured at the bottom of your news releases, included on your website and social platforms, and often used by the media. The person may want to include every detail about where they went to school or the job titles they held 20 years ago, but you need to be an advocate for trimming that material down to a concise, powerful summary of why they are the expert. A political candidate's love for their four dogs—complete with their breeds and names—doesn't necessarily need to be included.

THE TAKEAWAY ——————————————

To tell a good story, make sure you have an excellent angle. This will help focus your narrative and develop your supporting points, voices, statistics, images, and video.

Good options for angles include:

- person vs. thing—getting through conflict
- solutions to problems
- oddball stories
- evergreens
- localizing national trends

The best stories connect with emotions and give the reader or viewer information that's new, useful, and important.

DIY REAL-LIFE LESSONS: CHRIS ECCLESTON

"Capture emotion or engage the audience."

Chris Eccleston didn't plan to become a local media sensation or even a businessman. After serving in the US Navy as a nuclear plant operator leading 35 other sailors, he went into construction management as a civilian career path. While working his way through college, he developed the idea for a new venture after becoming frustrated with a lack of focus and mission orientation he encountered in the private sector. The eventual result was Delmarva Veteran Builders, a $25 million construction firm now on the Inc. 5000 list.

DVB has gotten a lot of media attention due in large part to Eccleston's style and approach to telling the company story—beginning with the name. "That was intentional, the veteran piece," he recalls. "The parallels are very similar between military and construction, in my mind. Couple that with attitude, the winning mindset—nobody's joining the military who doesn't have a service heart—all those things are there. . . . We contrast the average veteran—they wear a uniform, they show up, they have integrity—with a picture in your mind of the average contractor."

That's the DVB story in a nutshell. Not all its employees are veterans, but a good many are, applying the discipline and skills from their service to their work building schools, restaurants, gas stations, and more across a three-state region.

For Eccleston, every media hit is an opportunity to strengthen and reinforce his company's story. "It's an opportunity to gain brand awareness. It's not going to [immediately] translate to dollars for us," he observes. "Everything we do is intentional to try to capture emotion or engage the audience. . . . Our logo's very memorable, the graphics we use are very memorable."

Early local media coverage came from a simple initiative to win relevant awards. "I knew that would give me credibility as a new business," Eccleston says. "So we won the Chamber small business of the year, and then we won a [construction industry] membership award. . . . That would be a talking point for every new client or prospect. It gained momentum for us. . . . That winning got us press, and then we were front of mind so anytime there was a next [award] coming up, we were nominated because we had been in the press, and it just kind of created this huge cycle."

The pinnacle, he says, was receiving a national Secretary of Defense award: "I went to the Pentagon, and we got a bunch of media from that. It felt like we were on a 6-12-24-month run of being in the news."

His firm is branching out a bit into other related areas, including publishing a children's book incorporating DVB's values and an adopt-a-nonprofit program that will forge a partnership between the company and the nonprofit. "We believe we can learn from them about being resourceful and creative and having purpose and a mission, and we can teach strategy and leadership and all other kinds of things about business," Eccleston says. "I feel pretty confident that story and that cohort that will become part of the story will gain press attention."

— 4 —

WRITE IT SO THEY'LL RUN IT

One of the big secrets of local journalism is that a large number of the items you read in the newspaper or hear on the radio aren't written by a staff reporter or editor. Instead, they're crafted by a school principal, a franchise owner, or a garden club president, and the media prints or airs them without changing so much as a comma.

The authors of those stories probably didn't go to journalism school or work on their college newspaper. They may not even have gone to college. Their secret is the ability to read and listen to relevant stories in the news and then follow that style and format as closely as possible. What they send to editors and news directors is written so well that it can be used verbatim. All the media outlet has to do is copy, paste, and put a headline on it.

This practice has been common in local weekly papers for generations, and with staff reductions in recent years it's become more accepted as a way for larger daily papers to handle smaller news items. Just look for stories that run in your local paper without a reporter's name on them—or for photo credits that say "Submitted." Chances are excellent that those were provided by someone who wanted good PR for their organization and knew how to get it. If your release reads well, the local radio station will probably just rip and read it as its own.

Even television outlets may copy some of your language directly when writing their scripts and headlines.

This is a reality of the media today, and it creates a world of opportunities for getting your story out there.

One Way to Write

Writing is intimidating for a lot of people. It can be tough: Even experienced professionals with advanced degrees have been known to avoid writing memos or reports because they don't feel fully confident in their writing skills.

The good news about writing for public relations is that you don't have to fill your story with a lot of high-falutin' wordsmithing. You just have to explain your story at a sixth- to eighth-grade level, as simply and straightforwardly as possible. Make it easy to understand and your audience will eat it up.

There are many ways to approach writing, and this book can't possibly mention even half of them. But after more than 20 years of writing for a living, I've found an approach that works for me and might work for you too:

1. **BRAINSTORM** Begin by writing down whatever ideas come to mind about your topic, without self-censoring. Force yourself to keep the bad ideas. Write down words, phrases, numbers, sentence fragments, whatever bubbles to the surface. Don't delete or scribble anything out—that comes later. Just fill up a sheet of paper, or two, or three.

2. **FREEWRITE** Next, take those ideas and start writing something, anything about them. Set a five-minute timer and write until your time is up. Even if it's gibberish, just keep writing. Brainstorming is a way to get your mind generating ideas; freewriting is about generating words and sentences. (The concept was developed by educator Peter Elbow in his

1973 book *Writing Without Teachers*. If you're interested in learning more, pick up a copy—it's a powerful book.)

3. **RETHINK** Put your writing aside for a while and let your subconscious go to work on it. As your day or night goes on, more ideas will pop into your head, or you'll realize how to refine a concept or craft a sentence to make it more effective. If you're like me, the best ideas will arrive while you're away from your workspace, so carry a pocket notebook or use a mobile app to capture them so you don't forget.

4. **WORDIFY** (Yes, I made that word up.) Take the best of your ideas, words, and phrases and type them into a search engine to see what comes up. Run them through a synonym finder such as an online thesaurus. Based on what you find, take some time to improve and enhance your copy. Make sure you're not accidentally plagiarizing phrases; it may shock you that the phrase you were going to use as your lead sentence appeared in a presidential candidate's speech in 1988. Merge and meld your sentences to identify opportunities for alliteration, a very valuable tool of the trade. (Alliteration is best used sparingly, for emphasis—don't overdo it.)

5. **PACKAGE IT UP** This is what most people think of as "writing." At this step, you start putting down your words, fitting them into a particular format. If, for example, you're writing a news release, you want to include a headline, a sub-headline, the lead sentence and introductory paragraphs, curated quotes, and so on. Even if you still need to significantly edit it, the format helps make it real. Keep editing and refining throughout this process.

6. **DISCONNECT FOR A BIT** Working in PR and journalism, you're often under very tight deadlines that you can't control. But if you do have some flexibility, use it to take a nap or

go for a walk. Let your brain disengage entirely before giving your work another read. Don't try to crash the project into final form all in one sitting unless you absolutely have to. Your brain, and your readers, will thank you.

7. **ONE LAST EDIT** Give your story a final read. Nitpick the heck out of it. Do a final spelling and grammar check. If possible, get another human being's eyes on it, even if they're your partner's at home on a Tuesday evening. Once you're finished, submit.

And then start over on your next project with Step 1.

Writing Quotes

In a news story, the most important words are your lead, your explanatory paragraph, and the quotes from your story's subjects. You can accidentally sabotage your entire publicity effort with a few mediocre quotes—or create something that will get picked up by every paper around with a few good ones.

Good quotations in a news release are absolutely crucial. Every reporter and editor is looking for quotes that cut to the heart of an issue. Even if they're writing their own story on your organization instead of running yours, they may pluck a quote from your release to supplement their reporting. That's fair game—in fact, it's what you actually want.

You may be working with a hands-on CEO who drafts their own quotes, or a nonprofit director who wants you to write them all. It can be intimidating to write quotes to be attributed to different people, reinforcing key messages without duplicating content, but it's actually fairly easy to do. Here are some techniques to follow for success.

WRITE FROM THE TOP DOWN If you have several people quoted in a story, place them in order of importance, quoting the boss first and going in descending order from there. The exception is if you have a "real person" whose experiences help tell the story, such as a single mother who excelled in her electronics apprenticeship program and now can afford a better quality of life for her daughter—that quote should go at the top behind the lead sentence.

BRAINSTORM WORDS AND PHRASES Check for synonyms and historic or literary quotations that use relevant key words. Don't borrow others' words, but do use them for inspiration.

APPEAL TO EMOTION The bulk of your release will take the form of a basic news story, imparting information and facts. A quote is where emotion can come into play, with personal or community stories and powerful language that highlights the problems and solutions your organization is working on.

WRITE LIKE THEY SPEAK Spend some time listening to the person for whom you're writing a quote. Do they tend to ramble? Speak softly? Do they yell half their sentences? Are there phrases they like to use over and over? Try to mirror some of what you hear in the quotes you create for them.

MAKE IT LONG ENOUGH I've seen many releases over the years with just single-sentence quotes. If you're going to take the time to highlight a person and their thoughts, make it longer. I try to put three sentences in each quote, which typically does the trick. Here's my standard approach:

> **FIRST SENTENCE** Align it with your primary messaging and mission. Tell a story, if it fits the situation.

> **SECOND SENTENCE** Highlight supporting data or statistics, or include a call to action.

> **THIRD SENTENCE** The boring stuff—anything that your partners or your boss requires you to include. This often takes the form of thanking supporters or funders.

FOR EXAMPLE "I met a young lady last year who brought her grades up from an F to a B+ with the help of an after-school mentor. Young people need solid role models now more than ever, and that's why the Smithville Youth Network is seeking 300 adults in Smith County to step up and volunteer just one hour a week to mentor a child," said CEO Jane Smith. "We couldn't hold this networking fair without the support of our partners and funders, and appreciate their devotion to the cause of helping young people succeed."

You can even use the quote as a transition to segue from one topic or thought to another. That will give your final release a nice even cadence and flow.

A quote should not, under any circumstance, sound like a PR person wrote it. Here's an example of a poorly written quote:

Smithville ———————————————————————

"The Smithville Logistics team has accomplished extraordinary results for clients that consolidate their operations with our one-year-old Cohesion service," stated Joanna Johnson, senior executive vice president of southwestern sales operations and financing for Smithville Logistics. "Providing our clients with opportunities to modernize fleet, warehousing, shipping, and door-to-door delivery services through our unified, scalable management platform software yields noteworthy fiscal reductions and functional productivity increases. It's exciting to work for our clients and help them grow."

Unfortunately, that Frankenstein quote is very similar to the type of material you read in modern corporate news releases, put together by someone who doesn't write how they speak—or who doesn't listen well to how other people speak. It may actually have been written by a computer using a synonym search and a patchwork of artificial intelligence tools. No one is going to print that quote unless they're being paid to do so.

How can we write a better quote on the same subject? By being direct, specific, and above all, human.

Smithville

"Businesses in Smithville County kept telling us that they needed a single solution to their shipping problems, and that's what we gave them with the Cohesion service," said Smithville Logistics vice president Joanna Johnson. "One year after launch, we have more than 150 satisfied businesses uniting their warehouses, fleet trucks, customer shipping, and delivery services, saving an estimated $32 million each year. It's fun to come to work each day and help our clients grow by solving their logistics problems."

That quote is now a complete story. It leads with a specific customer problem, offers a clear solution, and details the results, all explained in a way that's understandable to someone from outside the industry (like reporters and editors). Smithville Logistics comes off as a hero, instead of putting the reader to sleep with a bunch of industry jargon.

The Elements of Writing for the Media

Those are the bigger-picture considerations. When it comes to crafting your actual piece, here are the key items to consider:

MATCH THEIR STYLE Read examples of good news writing—not from the *Washington Post* or the *New York Times*, but from your good local or regional newspaper or website. Pick up a copy of René Cappon's book *The Word* and read it cover to cover. (You'll find more resources in the Recommended Reading section at the back of this book.)

INCLUDE THE BASIC ELEMENTS Every journalism story should answer the questions who, what, when, where, why, how, and so what? (The latter is also known as "who cares?")

WRITE A SIMPLE, STRAIGHTFORWARD, PUN-FREE HEADLINE Copy the style of the media outlet you're sending to. Does it capitalize all major words in the headline, or just the first word? Avoid puns. Many reporters and editors love them, but often they don't work in a headline. A silly headline can trivialize and infantilize serious, important topics. Just be direct and plain and emphasize the importance of what you're doing.

CRAFT A CLEAN LEAD Your lead has to capture the reader's attention while including the most important information. It doesn't need to include all five w's, just the ones that matter the most to the story. For example, if you're holding a Christmas in July event, *when* might be the most critical part of the story, while *how* can be addressed a few sentences later.

USE SIMPLE, DIRECT LANGUAGE Don't bog your readers down with fancy rhetorical flourishes or flowery phrases. Make sure your explanatory information isn't too technical or complicated. News writing should be on a sixth- to eighth-grade level, simple and straightforward.

ELIMINATE JARGON Remember that the vast majority of local-news viewers and the print-reading public don't understand your organization's or industry's acronyms, inside jokes, or technical terminology. Cut those out wherever you see them.

WRITE TIGHT AND SHARP Cut out any words that don't add information, clarity, or depth. (Hint: In 90 percent of sentences, the word "that" can be eliminated without any clue it was ever there. In the sentence you just read, for example.)

PROVIDE PLENTY OF CONTEXT Statistics, history, and the reason or cause for your news announcement are critical. Explain to your readers why this issue is important and why they should care (the so what? part of the journalism basics, above).

DON'T FORGET THE DETAILS Include the time, date, location, and a contact number and email address. I read a calendar item once about a block party being organized by a local church. It included the date and time, but no address—not even a general location. Don't force your readers to do work to look you up and call or email, because most of them won't.

INCLUDE PHOTOS OR VIDEO A good, clear, high-resolution photograph can dramatically increase your story's chances of getting into print. Include a photo caption to minimize the amount of work the media has to do. I almost never attach the photo directly to an email, as that can bog a message down and not make it to recipients' inboxes. My practice is to upload photos to a cloud service that allows downloading and then include that link at the top of the news release. That simplifies the journalists' work significantly.

The Mysterious Inverted Pyramid

If you've taken a class in journalism or heard a reporter talk about the craft of writing, you may have encountered the inverted pyramid. Most journalists prepare their stories using this model. The inverted, or upside-down, pyramid is a way to organize a story to present the most important information first. Take a triangle with the point facing down. The top is now the wide "base" of the triangle, where you put the most critical piece of information, often very broad and general to catch the reader's attention. From there, you work your way down the list of details in order of importance. As you go down the inverted pyramid, the story narrows and provides more details at a smaller, more granular, less important level. It's been described as moving from what people *need* to know to what is nice to know.

Here's an example of a short item written in inverted pyramid style:

Smithville ——————————————————————————

Most taxpayers across Smithville County will pay 10 percent more on average in property taxes next year to help combat local cancer clusters, the County Council voted Tuesday.

The tax increase will pay for environmental cleanups needed to improve water quality that has been blamed for certain cancers in the county. It will go into effect in January.

The increase will not affect properties valued at less than $50,000, and small farms of less than 10 acres are also exempt. Taxpayers can file a hardship petition starting in August to request an additional exemption.

The council voted 5–2 to adopt the tax increase.

You don't need to remember what "inverted" means—just that you're writing the story with the most important information at the beginning and the least important information at the end.

Your Nut Graf

If you haven't worked in a newsroom, you've probably never heard the phrase "nut graf" before. "Graf" is just an abbreviation—newsroom-speak for "paragraph"—while the "nut" is a short, concise summary of your story, what makes it important, and why it matters. It's your story in a nutshell—a critical tool to help your reader instantly grasp the story. It's placed fairly high up, so that even if they don't read beyond that point, they still get the gist of what you're saying.

If you're writing a nut graf about a new produce stand opening up, your nut graf could be something like this:

Smithville

The stand is the first new farm stand to open in Smithville County in the last five years and will sell items like kale and sweet corn that aren't available at many other stands. It is the Smith family's second produce location outside of their main farm store.

That tells your reader why this particular stand is important (first new one in five years), what it means to readers (offers items they can't get elsewhere), and something interesting (the family expanding beyond its main farm operation).

What About Boilerplate?

"Boilerplate" language in a news release usually takes the form of a very dense paragraph of text following the body of your story, explaining what your organization or business is and does. If you really want to have a boilerplate paragraph, go ahead. You can also feel free to ignore it—most reporters certainly do. Your news release's nut graf and other details should explain enough about what you do to make a formal boilerplate statement completely unnecessary.

The Power of Headlines

The headline is the most important part of your story. That's not exaggeration or hyperbole; the headline is what catches the reader's eye in print or online and makes their eyes dip down and read more, or causes their fingers to click on a link. Without a good headline, there won't be many readers.

In public relations, your headline has to serve two purposes. The first is to catch the media's attention by being short, simple, and straightforward and containing actual news. The second is to catch the reader's attention once your headline is copied verbatim by the editor or producer. It needs to have interesting information and compelling emotion and be understandable by someone with no previous knowledge of the story or its details.

For examples of good headlines, I turned to the local newspaper where I cut my teeth as a copy editor for five years, the *Chronicle-Telegram* in Elyria, Ohio, one of the few remaining family-owned community newspapers. Here are a few examples from a recent online edition:

INFORMATIONAL: ODOT Sealing Cracks on State Routes 301 and 611 Next Week

> Plain and direct, this headline contains the critical details in one simple sentence: who (the Ohio Department of Transportation, or ODOT), what (sealing cracks), where (Routes 301 and 611), and when (next week). While jargon and abbreviations are generally frowned upon, in this case all the readers understand what ODOT is—and it's much simpler than the department's full name.

EMOTIONAL: "God Just Took Her Home and Made Her a Real Angel": Community Remembers Longtime Activist Dotti Washington

> This headline uses a powerful quote to memorialize and celebrate a person's life. The quote leads into the facts that readers need to know. It's longer than what we usually look for in a headline, but it perfectly showcases the emotion and feeling of loss in the story.

EVOCATIVE: Music Therapy to Soothe Patients' Souls at Mercy Health

> This simple story could just as easily have been headlined: "Hospital creates music therapy program," but the real headline simultaneously evokes a feeling of calm in the reader and shares the importance of the new initiative. The alliteration

with "soothe" and "souls" also creates a positive response in readers.

Some people write the headline last. That's typically how it's done in newsrooms: A reporter writes the story and sends it to an editor. The editor makes changes and sends it to a copy editor, print designer, or web producer, who writes the headline to fit space or attract the most clicks.

My general approach is to write the headline for my news release first. That gives my writing direction and focus and also provides my unconscious mind more time to mull it over and make changes. When I worked as a reporter, I put suggested headlines at the top of my stories to do the same thing. (Sometimes the copy editors used them, sometimes they didn't.) Try writing your stories both ways—headline first and headline last—and see what works best for you.

Imagine a Specific Person

This is a mental tool I used as a news reporter in a county of 200,000 people and again a decade later when I did PR for a school district in that same county. I would imagine specific, real people reading my stories and my news releases. I tried to put myself in their shoes picking up the local weekly paper and reading the headlines, or watching the 6 p.m. news and seeing an interview I'd just arranged. There was the community leader running a youth mentoring program, the second-generation firefighter in charge of a large fundraising event, the farmer who coordinated the Watermelon Queen program, the attorney who'd written a local history book.

That helped me focus my writing tremendously, to cut material that my imaginary panel of readers didn't care about and to add information that they'd consider essential for them and their families.

This perspective will become second nature as you get more experience. When you're just starting out, you may find it helpful to recruit your own real-life panel and share your drafts with them. Family members and employees may be too deferential and think you want praise, when what you actually need is raw feedback—so pick people who you know aren't going to just tell you what they think you want to hear. Ideally, your panel will point out areas or topics that you need to add, tell you that an entire paragraph isn't useful and can be deleted, or point out a confusing phrase. Get that feedback early in your writing process.

THE TAKEAWAY

When writing a news release or media advisory, clarity is more important than style. The simplest, most straightforward writing is often the best.

Here's a quick checklist of what you need to include:

- a solid headline
- strong quotes
- the most important information first
- a paragraph with context and background

There's no one correct way to write—there are many. Just make sure to get a trusted partner or coworker's eyes on the text before you send it to the media.

— 5 —

THE MEDIA

Smithville ————————————————————————————

Sarah Simmons has just been hired as principal of Smithville High School. One of her directives from the superintendent is to raise the school's profile and get better news coverage than the neighboring districts. Brand-new to Smithville, she doesn't know the people or the players well. Her first goal is to understand who the local media outlets are; learn about the reporters, editors, and producers; and figure out what kinds of stories might appeal to them.

Across the United States, there are fewer reporters, fewer editors and producers, and fewer media organizations reporting on local news today than there were even five years ago. The pandemic devastated the news industry on the local level as advertising levels plunged, newspapers merged, and publishers laid off hardworking journalists.

In 2000, when I got my first job in journalism, the total Sunday newspaper circulation in the United States was 59 million papers. Today, it's 25 million, according to the Pew Research Center. The number of people in newspaper newsrooms has been slashed by 57 percent since 2004, now sitting at just over 30,000. One way of looking at that math is that there's one newspaper journalist for every 11,000 people in the USA. Of course not every one of those 11,000 is going to do something newsworthy, but even so, the numbers are daunting.

Your local media outlets have suffered the same way. Listen to a local radio station's news broadcast. How many different reporters' voices do you hear today compared to a decade ago? Watch your 6 p.m. television news. The reporters there are likely younger, with less professional experience, than they used to be. And read your newspaper. It has fewer pages, fewer stories, fewer bylines—and may even be physically smaller, as page sizes themselves have been trimmed to save money.

It's been a decade since I worked in a newsroom, but I have immense respect for those who remain and persist. It takes a special kind of person to do that work to begin with, and they're under even greater stress now than they were in my time. This book isn't about gaming the system and tricking the media into covering your stories—it's about figuring out how to tell your story so the media will want to report it. The advice we're about to dive into will help both you and them.

Not Specialists, but "Glorious Generalists"

Most reporters—across all types of media—are not specialists in the fields they cover and do not usually have firsthand experience in their beat. Most food writers are not trained chefs. The vast majority of local reporters who cover zoning and development haven't bulldozed earth or cut down trees; many of them may not even own a house themselves. Business reporters typically don't have MBAs or degrees in finance, and odds are few have ever started their own company.

Reporters are, to borrow the words of educator and author Grace Llewellyn, "glorious generalists." They have the knack of learning a little information very quickly about a lot of different subjects. They soak up the fundamentals easily, picking up just enough of the background and terminology to be able to ask intelligent questions and then explain what they've learned to a broad audience. That's a critical skill, and one that's vastly underrated in today's specialist society.

During my years as a reporter, an average week might have looked like this:

MONDAY: Writing business profile of new ecotourism venture

TUESDAY: Covering county council meeting focusing on residential development

WEDNESDAY: Doing interviews for a feature article on the local search-and-rescue team

THURSDAY: Writing political story about very tense sheriff's race

FRIDAY: Working on story about sewer system expansion in rural communities

When I started out in journalism, I had no particular background in writing about tourism; didn't know a lot about the homebuilding industry; certainly had never gone on a search-and-rescue callout; had never worked on a political campaign; and most definitely didn't know a lot about sewers.

What I did have was the ability to ask questions in an intelligent way and put the information that I collected into a format that was understandable to the general public. Despite being an introvert, I rather liked talking to people and learning new things. That's a talent that all reporters have. Some reporters do focus on certain areas—not necessarily because of special training or education, but because they're just interested in a given topic.

I've known a lot of reporters who covered the court system very well, and none of them were attorneys. Simply put, they just sat, watched, listened, wrote, and learned over time. Occasionally you may find a former biology major covering science topics, or a military veteran reporting on the armed services—but they're relatively few and far between.

The flipside of that is also important: Just as reporters don't need a license or permit to practice their trade, PR practitioners don't need one to do their jobs either. There are no special access codes needed to talk to reporters. There are no passwords necessary to get inside the sanctum. You just need knowledge—the same type of know-how that reporters have—in order to reach the media.

That's what the rest of this chapter is all about.

Researching the Media

Once you have a good handle on your ultimate target audience, as detailed in the previous chapter, it's time to start investigating media outlets. Cast a wide net—but make informed decisions and don't just blast your message out blindly.

There are four basic categories of media outlet: print, TV, radio, and online. Today, many outlets cross those lines. Almost everyone has a website and dedicated social media channels, which means that even traditional print newspapers are also publishing stories online multiple times a day. Many medium or large papers produce video stories or news webcasts. And many outlets have podcasts as well.

The sections that follow will highlight what you need to know about each type of media operations in order to succeed.

LOCAL NEWSPAPERS Weekly, twice-weekly, or daily newspapers that cover local communities, these media outlets represent the backbone of American journalism. They provide news and information that people can't get anywhere else—at all. Their reporters typically cover more ground and report more deeply than other types of local media. They attend and write about meetings of city councils and school boards, cover everything from criminal trials to high-school sports in depth, and publish letters to the editor about traffic problems and people who don't pick up after their dogs. Their photographers snap pictures of people at the best and worst times in their lives. Local newspapers provide a lens on American politics, culture, and society that no other type of media outlet matches. Over the next few decades, many of these outlets may drop the "paper" part and go all online, like their hyperlocal website counterparts described below. But until then, there is no substitute for a good-quality local newspaper.

These outlets have also been harder hit economically than most other types of media, according to research from the University of North Carolina's Hussman School of Journalism and Media. More than 2,000 weekly or non-daily newspapers have been closed since 2004—about 100 a year—often shuttered after a large corporate ownership group buys out the local family owners. More than 6 percent of counties in the United States lack any newspaper at all, while half of all US counties have only one. This creates a local monopoly without the fierce competition that gave readers great news coverage decades ago. During the COVID-19 pandemic, more than 90 local news outlets closed, according to the Poynter Institute.

HYPERLOCAL ONLINE OUTLETS The decline of print journalism, combined with the increasingly low cost of running an online venture, has led to a cottage industry of highly localized, geographically centered news operations. Staff members who were laid off from newspapers, or whose papers were closed, have begun opening up such sites, often with foundation support, as one-person shops or team newsrooms. In my area, two hyperlocal outlets have sprung up in recent years—one is an advertising-driven network of sites featuring multiple writers with financial backing from a grocery-store owner, and the second is a solo operation using a subscription-based model. Both have produced some solid work.

COMMUNITY MAGAZINES These publications, often available for free at restaurants, checkouts, community centers, and other locations, are mostly advertising-driven publications with business and community profiles, feature stories, and trend articles. Some operate on a pay-to-play model—you buy an ad and get an article written about you—while others are more editorially independent. You'll have to do some research to find out what's available in your local area.

TRADE MEDIA Almost every business sector has a specialty publication or online magazine covering news, trends, people, and events. These can be e-newsletters with news roundups like the slate of industry-specific newsletters from SmartBrief.com, or narrowly targeted print magazines such as *Construction Executive* or *Progressive Grocer* to name just a couple. These magazines and newsletters often publish original content from businesses in their field that provide useful information and insights. An article placed in a trade publication can be leveraged for publicity in your local area—it builds your authority and reputation, can be used in customer marketing, and adds credibility when you pitch to a local editor.

LOCAL AND REGIONAL SPECIALTY PUBLICATIONS Look to your local newsstand, convenience store, or grocery-store checkout line for any magazines or other publications that might cover your story. These might include glossy, thick, ad-heavy city or state magazines; newspapers covering a particular recreational niche, such as hunting or boating; or consumer magazines on a particular topic, like destination weddings or home remodeling. Depending on your line of business, such a publication can be valuable to you because their audience may be exactly the audience you want to reach.

RADIO STATIONS Local radio news operations run the gamut from one-person rip-and-read studios—so called because they sometimes literally rip articles from the local paper and read them on air—to larger, highly sophisticated reporting and producing teams like those found at many public radio affiliates. If the station does independent reporting, the focus will be on tightly written pieces with multiple sound bites—so make sure you have short, pithy quotes ready to go when they interview you. A survey of radio news directors from a broadcasting industry trade group found more than 70 percent of stations broadcast local news, the rare case of a media channel expanding rather than shrinking.

LOCAL TV STATIONS Most local TV news operations are affiliated with one of the major national outlets—ABC, CBS, NBC, or Fox. They take their national news from the networks and produce newscasts full of local news. Reporters at smaller markets will often be there on contracts lasting a few years and then try to make their move up to a larger station in a bigger city. In recent years, field reporters who used to go around with a cameraperson in a large news van are now handling camera work on their own and driving less expensive compact cars. Instead of editors, they have producers who assign stories and plan and coordinate the newscasts. Often, both radio and TV outlets will take their lead from newspapers or hyperlocal sites, following bigger stories or finding local angles for their specific market. According to a broadcast media trade group, local news coverage hit new highs in 2019 and then again in 2020—in terms of both the number of stations airing local news and the number of hours devoted to it.

LARGER DAILY NEWSPAPERS Known as "major metros," examples include the *Boston Globe* or the *Chicago Tribune*. They cover larger metropolitan areas and surrounding suburbs and may have reporters in the state capitol and Washington, DC, covering local angles. If you're in one such paper's coverage area, then pitch your stories to them after doing some careful research to find the right specific reporters. If you're outside their range, don't waste your time.

THE GIANTS The big players in American media are the giants—*USA Today*, the *New York Times*, *Wall Street Journal*, *Washington Post*, *Los Angeles Times*, *New York Post*, CNN, ABC, CBS, NBC, NPR, and Fox. Each has a national focus and won't typically spend their time on local topics unless there's a juicy scandal or breaking news of special importance. If a reporter from one of these outlets gives you a call out of the blue or shows up at your event unsolicited, chances are you may be facing trouble. Unless you have a special unreported story that's of particular interest to a certain reporter at one of the giants—like a truly groundbreaking new way to solve the opioid crisis or a political lobbying effort that targets the Speaker of the House—then your time will be better served working with your local and regional media than trying to pursue these larger newsrooms.

Media Beats

Traditionally, reporters cover a particular "beat," a specific topic or geographic area that's their responsibility to report on. At the national level, beat reporters in New York or Washington might cover Wall Street, Congress, the airline industry, or the federal courts. Locally, you may have reporters who cover certain towns or counties or focus on business, entertainment, politics and elections, or the arts. That's less true with TV or radio reporters, who tend to shift between topics on a daily or even hourly basis. They may have geographic areas to cover, but their stories aren't often segmented by topic.

In recent years, I've seen an increasing number of journalists become general-assignment (GA) reporters. That means they're up for any story that arises that day—sometimes handed out by an editor, sometimes developed by the reporter. While GA reporters have more flexibility to cover breaking news or emerging trends, they also lack the depth of knowledge that a beat reporter has. Instead of a beat reporter who attends every town council meeting and thus will understand how the issue being debated today relates back to a story from last year, a GA reporter may drop in based on a call from a citizens' group, write a quick story, and leave. Their stories are generally more superficial and less insightful. But when an editor's staff is cut from 10 reporters to 5, they have to make decisions about coverage—and it may simply make more financial sense to not have reporters anchored to a specific beat.

Your Personal Media Ecosystem

Obtaining specific information on your local media outlets isn't hard. The information they use to sell themselves to potential advertisers is the same information you need to plan your public-relations approach.

To begin, contact the advertising team for the outlet in question and ask for a copy of their media kit and advertising rate information. That will include the details about the geographic areas they serve, how many readers or viewers they have, and sometimes also important audience demographics like age and income level. Some smart media outlets will have media kits easily available on their websites. You may have to sit through a call with an advertising rep who wants to follow up, but you're under no obligation to purchase ads from them. Buying advertising is a subject for an entirely different book, so we're just going to stick with PR here.

If you're dealing with broadcast, whether radio or TV, you should ask about their audience at different times of the day or numbers for specific programs, like the 6 p.m. news versus the 11 p.m. news. You also should ask for print, TV, and radio audience numbers separately from their online numbers. Many outlets' advertising arms will combine that into one number to make it more impressive if their traditional audiences are declining.

You can assemble that information in a simple spreadsheet like the one below. You can and should refer back to it and use it to estimate your eventual reach once they start covering your stories.

Smithville

MEDIA OUTLET	TYPE	READERS / VIEWERS / LISTENERS	DAY / TIME
The Smithville Sun	Print	3,200	Tuesday and Friday
smithvillesun.com	Online	4,100	daily
WDAS-TV	TV	13,000	7 p.m. newscast
wdastv.com	Online	27,000	Daily
WDSM FM	Terrestrial radio (as distinguished from online and podcast)	10,000	Local news every 30 minutes

IN ACTION: *To learn about the local media outlets that might cover Smithville High's programs and students, Principal Simmons started watching the local TV news, listening to the morning talk radio shows, subscribing to all the local newspapers, and searching for local-interest websites. She found that the area's two weekly newspapers had traditionally covered the school in the most* *depth, including printing the honor rolls, sending reporters to graduations, and writing features about new staff members and outstanding students. The local TV station usually sent reporters only when something big was happening and ignored the routine details, while the local radio station aired only a few items now and then. She invited one of the weekly newspaper reporters to a get-to-know-you meeting over coffee that gave the writer a chance to interview her about her plans as the new principal, and set up a walk-around tour with a TV reporter who was relatively new.*

Ad Sales and the Journalism Wall

As your business or organization becomes more prominent and gets more news coverage, you will be approached by sales representatives from the very same radio, TV, and newspaper outlets that are reporting on your work, asking you to advertise with them. I cannot emphasize enough that you are under no obligation to purchase ads from anyone. If doing so fits into your marketing plan and budget and makes sense, that's great. But there's no rule, spoken or unspoken, that requires you to.

Any ethical, honest news outlet will have a firm wall between the advertising sales team and the reporters, photographers, and editors on the news team. Ad sales should not influence news coverage and vice versa. (This isn't just a preference of some organizations. It's part of the Code of Ethics of the Society of Professional Journalists, the leading organization for working reporters, editors, and photographers. The Code calls on journalists to "deny favored treatment to advertisers, donors, or any other special interests, and resist internal and external pressure to influence coverage.")

Beware of So-Called Awards

One of the more dubious advertising ventures that local media outlets are increasingly undertaking is "readers' choice awards." These go under a variety of names, like "Best of _____" or "Top _____" or

"_____ Stars"—just insert your business sector or location. "Best Workplace" is another common theme. If you're nominated, there's usually a "public voting" period where readers, viewers, or listeners can cast their ballots online.

The categories are usually so narrowly drawn that there's only a handful of choices, and there's rarely transparency about the number of votes cast or how nominations were made. Winning "Best Talk Radio Station in Smithville County" doesn't mean a thing when you're the *only* talk radio station in Smithville County. I once worked for a county vo-tech school district chosen as the "top trade school" in an area. Our only competition was a community college in a neighboring county, so it was highly unlikely that the "voters" had any real knowledge about which was better. In some cases, I've seen multiple winners declared for a certain category.

If you're selected as a winner, you'll get a pitch from an advertising rep wanting to sell you on ad packages, banners, logos, and other purchases to celebrate your "award." If you're flush with cash and want a "Best of Smithville Winner" logo to put on your billboards and TV ads, then go for it—it won't hurt. But there's no evidence that it'll help, either. These are almost always advertising gimmicks—participation trophies with a veneer of respectability. Until media outlets start publicly disclosing the nominations process and the number of votes each contestant receives—just as the newsrooms do for real elections—then these "awards" have no real validity or value to you.

Reaching the Media

That decline in traditional journalism we talked about earlier makes your job both easier and more difficult. There are fewer reporters to reach, but the outlets that remain are still looking for good material that they can run as easily as possible. Reaching the media is an art form in itself, but it's also pretty simple with some focus and organization.

ASSEMBLE YOUR LIST How do you find out reporters' names, email addresses, and phone numbers? Quite simply, you read the paper and scan the website. Most make it easy for you to contact their staff by putting that information at the end of each reported story. Toss all those items into a spreadsheet and make notes about what each person covers, when their stories run, how long the stories tend to be, what towns they report from, and whatever other details you can gather.

This method works for national reporters as well as local ones. If you're trying to reach someone with NPR, figure out what the typical NPR email address format is and use that to reach a staffer who has an unlisted email. Same with the big television networks, only there you look for the producers' names. LinkedIn is a great professional search tool and can often get you personal email addresses as well. A paid LinkedIn subscription is a little pricy, but it unlocks a lot of useful contact information that's not visible to users of the free site, so a subscription might be worthwhile.

If you can't find contact information online, don't despair. Just pick up the phone and call. After all, it's how it was done for years before "online" became a thing.

DO YOUR RESEARCH Once you've created your spreadsheet, it's time to dig a little deeper into the key contacts you've identified. Begin with a basic online search. Find out what each of your local journalists usually write about. Some may focus on a particular beat by geography, while others concentrate on a topic like business or education. You can often tell very quickly from scanning a reporter's stories what their personal interests are and how those influence their work. Some love writing about local musicians, while others prefer cryptocurrency. Their colleagues may cover education by going into local classrooms and writing a lot of feature stories, rather than digging into test scores and data. That's all very useful information when you're trying to pitch them.

Discover where they worked and lived previously, where they went to school, and what they did before journalism. Your veterans' club will want to know that a particular reporter served in the Marines, or your political organization could find it useful to know that an editor used to write about politics before she got a promotion. You can use that as a touchstone to start a conversation and build a relationship.

I've had many great chats with reporters with just the basic "who-do-you-know" conversational game, discovering common ties through college or previous jobs (LinkedIn is great for this kind of information). Even the simplest of chats can give me insight into what they're interested in or how they might think about a story.

Once you've had that talk, don't hesitate to ask them point-blank what types of stories they are interested in—and what specific stories they may be working on. That reporter who covers education may not ever write a feature about your PTA's fundraiser because it's seen as too small. But he might be very interested in a trend story about PTAs using online fundraisers or crowdsourcing to help support their local schools—so that's the story that you pitch, with you at the center.

As former editor of the *Riverfront Times* newspaper in St. Louis, Missouri, Sarah Fenske estimates she received thousands of pitches. Of those, often only "one or two were good," she says. "Relevant to our local audience, super timely, and with a note of controversy or conflict."

For Greg Bassett, editor of the *Salisbury Independent,* a weekly newspaper in Maryland, it's all about three words: "Local. Local. Local." He turns away items constantly, including opinion pieces from Washington, DC, think tanks "who don't seem to understand that I won't run their columns."

Editors and reporters have to sort through a huge amount of garbage to get to the gems. Your job is to make it as easy for them as possible—by ensuring your news pitch is one of those rare jewels.

KNOW WHAT THEY NEED Each type of media outlet has a different fundamental need; it's your job to help them meet that need with your stories:

> **A DAILY NEWSPAPER WANTS URGENT NEWS** to fill the next day's paper as well as bigger-picture, longer stories for the weekend, when fewer people are working in the newsroom.

A TELEVISION STATION NEEDS VISUALS. You can have a great story, but it won't air if there's nothing to show, see, or do. Make sure you set them up for success.

A RADIO STATION ALWAYS REQUIRES VOICES from the people at the center of the story. Get those interviews scheduled as soon as possible.

If you can't meet those basic needs, wait to pitch your story until you can.

DISTRIBUTE YOUR STORIES Once you have a story planned out and written, your interviewees selected and trained, your timing secured, and your visuals in the bag, then you need to get the word out to the media.

Contrary to what many PR firms will try to tell you, this isn't rocket science. It's not hard at all. Here's how to succeed, one step at a time:

STEP 1: Go back to the media list you assembled previously. You should have it in a spreadsheet so it's easy to sort and figure out who you want to send your news release to.

STEP 2: Paste the text of your release into the body of your email. Include all the important elements—contact information, links to photos or video, and a sharp, crisp headline in the subject line of the email.

STEP 3: Once everything is formatted properly in the body of your message, copy the email addresses of your selected media outlets into the bcc: field. (Do not use the cc: field. Do not ever, ever use the cc: field.) Bcc: means blind carbon copy, so no one will see their email addresses but you as the sender. If you slip up and use cc:, then everyone will see a bunch of competitor addresses at the top instead of your perfect lead. (In a truly worst-case scenario, you've just put everyone at risk of entering "reply-all" hell.)

STEP 4: Give it a close read one more time. Make any last-minute edits.

STEP 5: Hit send. You're done.

Don't Pay for a Distribution Service

A word of caution: There are several large companies that promise to send your news releases out to the media for a princely sum of money. They vow to eliminate the stress and hassle by sending your release out to a targeted list of journalists just salivating to write about you and handling the rest of the process for you as well.

That's generally a bunch of hokum. For a local or regional organization or business, those paid distribution services are generally a giant waste of money. Unless you're a very, very large organization seeking a national audience, there's no need to use them. You can do it yourself.

There's also no guarantee that these expensive paid services are reaching the reporters and editors you want to reach. When I was in a newsroom covering county and local governments, my inbox was routinely filled with releases about new purses, food products, and high-tech gadgets. I've never written a story about a purse in my life, yet someone at PurseCo Inc. was paying good money for me to get that news release. That's a colossal waste of resources.

You can easily do it yourself if you're smart and organized.

Email, Fax, or Carrier Pigeon?

When I started out as a reporter all the way back in 2000, we got a lot of news submitted by fax machine, creating piles of paper that we had to sort through hourly. I recall getting good stories just because I was standing near the fax when a release came through. At that time, the company didn't have email; I had to use my personal email address to get and share information with sources.

Today, no one should be using a fax machine to send a news announcement. (In fact, fewer and fewer businesses even have a fax machine anymore.) Emails and phone calls are the way to contact journalists. When in doubt, "email, always," says Fenske. Phone calls can be tricky. If you call at a good time, you can catch an editor ready to listen; if it's a bad time, they will want to get you off the phone as quickly as possible, or you'll end up in voice mail. Don't call to follow up or check in on the status of your release—that will just annoy anyone in a busy newsroom.

Timing Is Everything

Journalists are just like normal people. They want to have an easy week, do good work, and go home at the end of the day. They don't like it when a big story breaks at 3:30 p.m. on a Friday, or when they have to fight and dig for every little piece of information.

My rule of thumb is to send out news releases and pitches in the morning, as early in the week as possible. Later in the day can get your email buried in the in-box; later in the week and your story may well be lost under an onslaught of assignments from the journalist's editor or news director.

That said, some weekly newspapers have off-kilter production schedules—a paper that comes out on a Friday may be edited and designed on Tuesday. Be aware of your local news cycles and adjust your timing accordingly.

Television stations generally have a morning news meeting where assignments are given out. In my neck of the woods, that happens around 9 a.m., so I try to get my emails out by 8 a.m. to give the staff enough time to read and digest them.

Don't wait until the late afternoon, let alone the evening or weekend. News items sent then are almost guaranteed to be ignored. Even if that's when you have free time, your recipient is probably off the clock and not wanting to think about work. "Sending anything to a busy editor outside of working hours is the worst time to send anything," says Bruce Bishop, chief photographer for Ohio's *Chronicle-Telegram*. "I get so many messages, and I manage 80 percent of my time on my iPhone, so things drop down that list very fast. If I'm at work, the odds of it not being forgotten about or lost in a sea of spam are much higher."

Off-Limits Information

If your news is big, urgent, or truly complex, you may want to let reporters know about it ahead of time—which is to say, before the official announcement. That gives the reporter time to do their research, come up with intelligent questions, and assemble a rough story before you break the news widely. In return, they agree that they will keep it confidential. That kind of advance notice is called an embargo. Embargoes are more common in the world of business or technology, or when working with market-moving news like government economic data (or a new Marvel movie). Reporters are given the information a certain amount of time in advance with the promise that they won't report it until the agency or company formally puts the word out at a specific time.

Embargoes should be used fairly sparingly in the local news arena. Most of the time, there's simply no need to do an embargo. You also don't want to get a reputation for thinking that your news is as big as federal unemployment statistics or the newest Apple device.

That said, there are times when it may come in handy, especially on a selective basis with specific reporters. In this book's introduction, I told the story about those invasive beetles and how we handled the story at my then job with the state's agricultural agency. My agency was working with our federal counterpart on an announcement that this nasty invasive insect had been found in the state. The topic (and our solution) was somewhat complicated, so we gave a heads-up the day before to a local environmental reporter with the understanding that she would not write about it until our formal news release the next morning. When we sent that release out, her story was up online within a matter of minutes—fully reported and providing the context that we had hoped for. Because she was the state's preeminent expert journalist covering the environment and ecology, other media outlets looked to her story for guidance and took their lead from her.

That's a selective embargo that worked well for everyone. And it worked for the following reasons: She was a trusted journalist whom we'd worked with before and crucially, and she agreed to the embargo before we shared the story. If you blast out a news release to your entire media list and call it an embargoed release, then no one has to abide by that and you may get scooped on your own news.

Exclusives

An exclusive is a cousin of the embargo, under which you give your story to just a single reporter. The advantage of an exclusive is that you can sometimes secure prominent placement in a larger news outlet by promising they're the only one you're giving the story to; every media outlet likes to have something the others don't. That said, editors or producers won't negotiate with you about when and where it will run—they reserve that decision for themselves—so your hope of a page A1 story in your major metro paper may be dashed. The disadvantages of an exclusive arrangement are that you may anger other reporters to whom you didn't show favor and that those other outlets may be less interested in covering a story that's already appeared exclusively elsewhere. Backlash can be very real when you're working with exclusives because you are essentially picking and playing favorites.

Use exclusives even more sparingly—and strategically—than embargoes. Consider very carefully if it's worth it.

THE TAKEAWAY

Understanding how the media works is essential to getting your story featured in print, online, or on the air. Don't get suckered into paying thousands for a database of contacts or a distribution service. Here's how to DIY it:

- Read, listen, or watch your local media outlets (and follow individual reporters' work) to know what they like to cover.

- Put contact information, circulation or audience, and other details into a spreadsheet, then just copy and paste a column of email addresses when it's time to send your news.
- Time your releases just right—usually on a Monday or Tuesday morning, but check your local papers' deadlines first.
- Connect with reporters in real life at events and on social media.

Remember that many local reporters today are generalists not working a narrow beat. They're starved for time and probably being pressured to produce by editors and producers, so make things as easy as possible for them.

DIY REAL-LIFE LESSONS: GREG STAR

"How do reporters get to talk to all these people?"

When Greg Star and Mac Nagaswami launched what would become their national advertising firm Carvertise almost a decade ago, neither had any idea what they were getting into. They didn't know how to build buzz or get media attention—and that actually worked to their advantage.

Carvertise is based on a simple concept—the company pays drivers to wrap their personal vehicles in ads promoting colleges, products, marketing campaigns, and national brands. The advertisers get their eye-catching ads seen on the road, where many Americans spend a lot of their day driving for work or commuting to or from work. But at the start, Star says, "We didn't know anyone or anything."

They did know that they needed media coverage to build interest and get their start-up known. "One thing I looked at was, 'How do reporters get to talk to all these people?'" Star says. He learned that the governor's public schedule contained a list of media events and press conferences that would draw reporters—and he just started showing up. "Anyone can go!" he says. "You're showing your face, you're meeting people, you're talking to people. You meet other reporters, and it was so fun. I really didn't know any better! So I just kept going to places."

The early media interest in this new venture led to more attention, and that caught the interest of advertisers and the state's political leaders. "The thought was that these are our leaders. They want to grow entrepreneurship," Star recalls. "Our company also pays people to put ads on their cars, so people are also earning money. If we win, you also get a success story!" One of those early events also led to an eventual business partnership with the state housing agency to promote its homeownership programs, one of Carvertise's first government clients and a big get at the time.

Talking to reporters is nerve-racking, Star admits. His advice: Be as straightforward and open as you can. "It's hard, because you're nervous around reporters. You don't want to say anything stupid. But I'm very transparent," he says. "Just talk to them like humans. The point is not to think about the interview, but trying to build a relationship with this person for the long term. You don't want to be shortsighted like, 'Let me just get press.' Here is someone you want to connect with for five, ten years."

And it worked. Carvertise now has a national reach. It's grown far beyond its home state of Delaware, where it's still headquartered. Star spends most of his time on the road, crisscrossing the country to set up new campaigns and work with an ever-increasing number of clients.

– 6 –

THE DETAILS

Smithville

Amira Kadir has operated the Smithville Martial Arts Studio for just over a year. While there are no other martial arts programs in town, she's found that she's battling strong competition from other youth activities, such as soccer, baseball, Scouting, and dance classes. To get attention for her studio, she's planning a martial arts demonstration day in a local park next month, where her students will show off what they've learned and her instructors can teach some simple techniques to people who stop by. She's now trying to figure out how to get media attention, bring people out, and maximize coverage of the event.

The devil's in the details, and that's nowhere more true than in public relations. Even if you have a story that makes people cry or open their wallets, when working with the media you must also have the details right—from the small things to the big ones.

In a small organization or business, that will fall to you. There is no backup. Luckily, you have this book to help you get it right.

Do Your Research

Above all, your story has to be thoroughly researched and fact-checked. Don't leave anything to chance or assume that someone else has done the work.

Look into the backgrounds of people who have a great tale to tell. Make sure they're who they say they are, live where they say they do, and have done the things they claim to have done. Many organizations have been burned by people with tear-jerking stories that turn out to be completely false, such as military imposters who claim service that they never performed and medals they were never awarded. Don't get so caught up in the tale that you ignore your Spidey-sense. Ask polite but specific—maybe even difficult—questions that can confirm the person's narrative.

Research and verify any statistics and data points that you'll be using to tell your story. Too often, people who are embedded in an industry come to internalize certain data that may become exaggerated or vague over time and may not tell the whole story. They may say that more than a third of farmers in your county own fewer than 50 acres of land, when in fact the numbers are 27 percent and 40 acres. You need to confirm any numbers and make sure they're correct.

When you're telling a story to the media, it has to be 100 percent true in all respects. This affects the very integrity and soul of your organization or business. You can be vague about certain elements or gloss over precise details, but you must be accurate and truthful.

Managing Your Partners

Especially in the nonprofit or government worlds, you'll find yourself working closely with partner organizations or agencies. These may be groups that do similar work to yours, agencies that regulate your sector, or foundations that fund your work directly. To avoid upsetting long-standing relationships and possibly affecting future funding, you need to ensure that partner relationships are properly maintained and precisely finessed.

What does that have to do with public relations?

Many partners are very sensitive to media coverage. They like to control their public profile—just as you do—and want to ensure that they're represented in the best light possible. Funding organizations, whether they're foundations or government agencies, can be very particular about their portrayal in the press. They may insist on having veto power over the exact language used in a news release announcing the funding, for example—and they should! It's their money and their terms. Organizations whose work complements yours will want to make the distinctions between you and them clear so potential supporters understand the differences.

Working with Kids

Any organization that works with children has to be very careful when planning a publicity campaign. Kids need special protection from the impacts of news coverage, and there are a host of considerations regarding privacy and parental permissions to keep in mind. Photos require special handling. And children have to be specially prepared for talking to the media. Here are a few critical areas to plan for:

PERMISSIONS Whether you're a youth-serving nonprofit or a local school, you should have media forms on file for all participants but particularly students. These forms should be signed by parents or guardians and give permission for the organization and any media outlets to use the names, identifying information such as hometown and age, and photos or videos of each child. You can easily find templates online for these forms and customize them to your particular situation in consultation with your attorney. Best practice is to update these forms annually (you don't want to be like one organization that had been using a form for so long that it talked about sending the form by mail, fax, or telegram . . . but not email!). Be aware that some parents don't want their children's names published anywhere, and that needs to be respected. Make sure you have an up-to-date list of kids whose guardians declined and refer back to it whenever you get a media inquiry or do an event. This isn't just a matter of being camera-shy—you don't want a child whose parent is fleeing an abusive partner to end up in the background of a shot on the evening news or quoted in a story about after-school programs.

PRIVACY Sharing stories about clients or customers can be a great way to talk about your mission and accomplishments, humanize your organization or business, and cut to the core of your story. But their stories ultimately belong to them and are not entirely yours to tell. When working with children's stories, you need to be especially deliberate and careful that the parents or guardians are informed about and understand the implications of media coverage. Children can be especially vulnerable when their stories are shared, and for organizations that deal with special populations (such as kids with disabilities, crime victims, undocumented immigrants, and so forth), that doubles the potential negative impacts. Talk with your legal team and any subject-matter experts such as counselors you may have on staff to develop clear procedures and policies.

PHOTOS Media outlets love photos and videos of kids. Kids playing in the snow, studying in a classroom, competing in a game, going on a nature hike—those are all great visuals. In the Internet Age, however, those innocuous photos can go online and spread quickly to audiences far beyond your local publications or stations. In addition to making sure you have explicit written permission (above), you should do a basic check to ensure that any kids who are going to be featured are dressed and groomed properly for the weather and the event. You don't want to accidentally expose a child to ridicule because their shirt has a stain or a hole, or they're not wearing a coat in the cold. Also ensure that they have any necessary safety gear. It's easy to overlook basic protocols in the excitement of setting up a front-page photograph, but you don't want to expose kids in the after-school carpentry program to danger by forgetting to have them wear safety goggles.

INTERVIEWS Kids don't have the natural caution and filters that (most) adults do. They'll talk about anything to anyone, even if it's embarrassing, inappropriate, or highly personal. If you have identified kids in advance who are going to be interviewed, take the time to do a little preparation with them. Explain what the reporters will be asking about, make some gentle suggestions about things they could say, and offer some advice about topics to avoid. You should also explain how the interview will be held—will the reporter have a TV camera, a pen and notepad, or a still camera? (This may also help keep the reporter from encountering a group of children who instantly freeze and clam up at the sight of a camera.) You can't ensure that a kid won't spontaneously yell out "My mom has a big butt!" but you can do your best to keep them on-message.

Educating Reporters

Sometimes you'll have to do some work to educate reporters about specific terminology or critical details that they might otherwise misunderstand. Karen Foster, whom we'll meet again in Chapter 8, runs a nonprofit that serves persons with disabilities. After one article that included outdated, potentially offensive language such as "handicapped," she worked with the local editor to explain just why that was problematic. "She was really grappling with why we don't call people 'handicapped,'" Foster recalls. "Because of the opioid crisis, we were able to draw this parallel between how you don't refer to people as addicts, you refer to them as people with addiction. She really got it, and she was able to get us there."

Now, she has a one-pager on hand about the best ways to speak about disabilities that she can hand to a reporter. "Often, they just don't know," Foster says. "I try to give them this style guide so they know what words to use, and I haven't had a problem since."

Smithville

IN ACTION: *Amira Kadir has made certain to get photo, video, and media consent forms signed by her martial arts students' parents and guardians. She's explained to them that the media might be interested in talking to their kids, and talked with the students about the kinds of questions that reporters might ask them. She's also identified a handful of students at multiple levels of her program who would have especially good stories to feature, including a young man who was bullied, found the courage to stand up to his tormenter, and then invited the bully to study alongside him at Amira's school.*

Start Your Own Stock Library

Newspapers need photographs. TV stations need video. Radio stations need audio. And online outlets need all the above.

When you have a story to tell, of course you'll create those elements to support your specific narrative. But you should also have on hand a cache of general material that tells your organization's overall story if the media comes calling. When reporters are in a hurry, you need to be ready to give them what they need—and fast. Having a good, high-resolution photo of your executive director or company founder ready to go may just land their face on page one. And be sure to update those regularly! A 1980s headshot of your CEO with big hair and epic shoulder pads won't exactly build confidence that you're a modern, with-it organization.

Examples of this type of material include the following:

PHOTOS   Professional headshots of nonprofit executives and key officials

High-resolution studio shots of your products

Images of students in the classroom, workshop participants, volunteers, etc.

VIDEO CLIPS   Activities and programs in action
                   Major events, conferences, or trainings

In the broadcast media, stock video footage like this is called B-roll. This typically has audio tracks removed so that the media can just splice it into their stories without any significant editing.

If you're inheriting an existing PR program, you may already have some of these files on hand. You may just need to update them to reflect the current state of affairs. Organize your content so that it's easily findable when you need it in a pinch.

When I worked for a school district that was lobbying for funding for a major building project, we had to make the case that the current building was long past its prime. We couldn't bring the media into certain spaces without proper equipment and a significant time investment, so I brought those spaces to them.

I worked with the facilities staff to get video footage and photos of the boiler room, where the outdated and overwhelmed HVAC systems were located. For visual interest, I shot photos and video of the district superintendent and facilities chief inspecting monitors and equipment. I also climbed up to the roof to capture our leaky, many-times-patched flat roofs and got close-up images of crumbling brickwork on the outside of buildings.

I then created photo folders, edited together a silent video showing a school falling apart, and sent links to the media along with a news release on our efforts. The story got wide coverage in our target market, and the TV news used my footage to show what its cameras weren't able to capture.

Time-consuming? Absolutely. But worth it in every respect.

Tidy Up Your Desk

Reporters often like to interview people in the workplace. For many interviewees, that means in their office. Take 60 seconds before they arrive and tidy that key surface: stack your papers, straighten your in-box and out-box, and remove the remnants of your lunch. The cleanup job will make your organization look more professional, and for on-camera interviews it will focus attention on you and your words, not a messy or cluttered desk. If you're doing a virtual interview, check your background—a non-distracting, plain wall behind you is best. Don't use a virtual background or screen-blur feature, as that may produce odd effects.

Also: Stick anything personal or confidential out of sight or under cover. That isn't paranoia. Some of the nation's top investigative reporters, such as Seymour Hersh, Bob Woodward, and Carl Bernstein, got scoops by reading documents upside down while conducting interviews. Good reporters notice everything.

Answer Your Phone

Responsiveness is vital. Whether you're sending out a story or responding to an incoming inquiry, you have to return calls promptly. If the media calls, it's your responsibility to answer. If you're on vacation or sick or on a business trip, you delegate that to someone else until you're back at your desk. Your day doesn't end at 5:00 p.m.; it can go into the evening and weekends and can start as early as any given reporter wakes up.

You absolutely must be available directly after putting out a news release; it defeats the purpose of promoting a story if reporters can't reach you with questions or for interviews. If you send out a story on a Tuesday morning—an optimal time for reaching the media—then you need to clear your schedule and your spokesperson's schedule for most of the day Tuesday and Wednesday. There will invariably be a reporter who doesn't get assigned the story until a day or two afterward, and they'll want the same access that your first-day reporters received.

Assemble Your Media Kit

The phrase "media kit" can conjure up the image of a glossy folder with sheets of paper tucked into the pockets and a business card stapled to the cover. Today, the format has gone electronic, but the core pieces still remain. A good media kit accompanying an announcement or similar news story can leverage your organization's story and tell its backstory in the way you want it told.

A media kit can include photos and B-roll, as discussed above. It should also feature any statistics on the topic, represented in a graph or chart if at all possible. A good media kit will include prior coverage of the topic, a fact sheet conveying basic information at a glance, and a chronology of the issue at hand from start to finish. It can include bios of your leadership or company executives, if relevant. Quotes or testimonials from third-party endorsers can also help your cause.

Advise Them in Advance

When putting on an event just for the media—whether it's a formal news conference or a more informal groundbreaking or ribbon-cutting— you need to give them plenty of notice. Reporters and editors can be a forgetful bunch, battered as they are by the day-to-day whims and vagaries of the news business. My general rule of thumb is to send a media advisory at least a week in advance to let them do some research and put it on their calendars, and then follow up the day before with a second email as well as phone calls to the people I really want to be there.

A media advisory is a simple document outlining the who, what, when, where, why, and how of the event. You want to set the hook for reporters, sparking their interest to get them to attend. An advisory is different from a calendar item because it's intended for the press rather than the general public.

Advisories are generally understood to be used for planning purposes only, but proceed with caution: There will occasionally be an unscrupulous or sloppy media outlet that will take the information in your advisory and write a story from it. Don't include any details in the advisory that you don't want shared just yet.

Look for examples of media advisories in the Appendix.

Smithville

IN ACTION: About four weeks before the event, Amira sent out a first press release promoting it—written for her local newspapers and structured so that they could run it word for word. The week before, she sent out a media advisory just for reporters, editors, and producers, reminding them that the event was happening, listing possible photo and video opportunities, and mentioning a few of the students' stories. She's gotten nibbles from the main newspaper and the local TV station.

Write a Great Subject Line

Research has shown that a good email subject line is critical to getting a customer to open your email marketing pitch. The same is true for getting journalists to open your news releases and advisories. The subject line has to catch their attention quickly and get them to click and read more. Here are some key points to keep in mind:

DON'T REPEAT YOURSELF Your subject line shouldn't copy the headline of your release verbatim, but you should cut it down to the essential parts.

KEEP IT VERY SHORT Remember that most readers will see only a small part of the subject line in their email program—you want to have the most important information seen. There are multiple free online preview tools that can help you trim things down.

ELIMINATE EXTRA WORDS Don't clutter your subject line with phrases like "News Release" or "School News." The subject line itself should be enough.

BE PRECISE Avoid spammy words like the ones you find in your junk mail folder—"free," "rewards," "congratulations," "offer," "winner." You don't want your story to get flagged as spam before the recipient even sees it.

Real Stories from Real People

Which is more interesting to read?

(A) *The Smithville Youth Swimming Club will be expanding next year to add two new programs for younger swimmers, club President Jenny Smith said Tuesday. "The growing interest in swimming among this new generation made us realize we need more capacity to serve the population," she said.*

(B) *Marty Ellis knows how important a good community swim team is: Three of his four kids are on swim teams sponsored by the Smithville Youth Swimming Club. The fourth, at age six, is too young. That's why Ellis was excited Tuesday with the announcement that the club would be expanding to add two new programs for younger swimmers next year.*

The first is just a standard announcement by an organization. There's nothing really *wrong* with it, but it could be better. The second version adds a real person and shows how the initiative will solve a problem or improve their kids' lives.

"Real people" is a shorthand phrase used in journalism and PR to refer to clients, customers, students, and the like who can speak about their experiences with your programs or products. They're special because they don't have any other relationship with you—they're not on your staff or otherwise drawing a paycheck from your organization. Having real people to talk about the importance and impact of your work is a vital part of a media outreach effort. They are the best third-party validators for the media.

However, these real people can't just ramble on about whatever pops into their minds. If you're giving their names to reporters to interview, or if you're having them speak at a media event, they have to have good, solid stories. Do a preliminary interview first to make sure that's the case. Explore each story and see where all the rabbit holes lead. And do your due diligence by checking these people out to make sure they don't have anything in their backgrounds that could embarrass you.

This isn't just PR paranoia. Consider the case of former presidential attorney Rudy Giuliani, who held a news conference complaining of voting problems in Pennsylvania after the 2020 election and featured a poll watcher talking about his experiences. That poll watcher turned out to be a perennial political candidate—and convicted sex offender. There's no need to sully the good name of your organization or business by putting someone out there that you don't want to touch with a 10-foot pole.

Making Your Pitch

"Pitching" can be an intimidating term; it certainly was for me when I moved from journalism to PR. I did not look forward to trying to persuade reporters to write about my story of the day, or verbally arm-wrestle editors into running my op-ed.

That's in large part because I didn't feel like I had a good idea of what "pitching" was, even after working as a reporter and editor for more than a decade. I had covered county government, local business, courts, and other related topics, not a national beat like technology or fashion or politics. There weren't many PR staffers calling me up to convince me to write a story. I got plenty of friendly emails and reminder calls about events, but no one ever twisted my arm to get me to cover their story or run their column.

As it turned out, those emails and calls were actually pitches. And once I realized that, I also realized that I didn't need to do any forceful convincing. I just needed to tell a good story—and so do you.

Here's the basic information you need to have in hand when you put together your pitch. You'll modify it to fit your exact circumstances, of course, depending on whether you're proposing a trend story, trying to get reporters to attend an event, or just interesting them in your organization.

WHO?   Who is taking part in the event; who is affected by the news?

WHAT?   What, precisely, is happening or will happen.

WHEN?   The date and time of the event, or the timing of the story generally.

WHERE?   The location of the event, or the geographic area affected by the news.

WHY?   Why are you holding the event, or why is this announcement being made?

HOW?   How is the decision, program, or organization carrying out the details?

SO WHAT? Why is this important in the grand scheme of things? Why would readers of this publication or viewers and listeners of this station care?

If you have that information at your fingertips when making your calls or sending your emails, you'll dramatically increase your chances of getting news coverage. You would be surprised by the number of local announcements that editors receive lacking one or more of those basic elements. The most frequently missing item is the so what?, or why this news matters. Many people can't articulate that; if you can, you'll be heads and shoulders above the rest.

Pitching stories has gotten more difficult locally as the ranks of reporters have shrunk. As we've discussed in prior chapters, more reporters are on "general assignment" than are assigned to a specific beat, which means any given reporter might be taking whatever stories arise from day to day. GA reporters are often looking for quick-hit stories that have multimedia opportunities, quantifiable impact, and powerful personal testimonials. You can't count on their institutional knowledge or even that they've checked their own files to know the background. You have to explain the context from the start as part of your pitch.

THE TAKEAWAY

To maximize your impact, you must master the details when you approach the media. One incorrect fact or bad photo can hurt your organization. The top things to remember:

- Carefully manage relationships with your partners, such as funders or government agencies.
- Develop plain-language permission forms for parents or guardians to sign when working with kids, and make sure the adults understand exactly what's happening.
- Educate reporters on sensitive topics or language to avoid.
- Respond quickly when a reporter calls—don't put it off.
- Tell real stories from real people.

By the time you make your pitch, you need to have all those items sorted so actually talking with the media is the easiest part.

DIY REAL-LIFE LESSONS: KATHIE KLARREICH

"Bring that voice out to the public"

Kathie Klarreich is a former reporter, an author, and an international journalism trainer. She has a depth of experience working in the media that few others possess; her work has appeared on or in *Time*, the *New York Times*, the *Christian Science Monitor*, ABC, NBC, and National Public Radio.

In 2014, she applied several years of experience teaching writing to women in prison to found Exchange for Change, a Florida-based non-profit organization designed to connect students on campus with students in a prison, reading the same work—a short story or essay—and then exchanging their responses. "We paired them up, and that began a conversation between two writers in different institutions which lasted the entire semester," she says. "Our mission is twofold. One is to go inside and bring communications skills through writing, and the second is to bring that voice out to the public. Unless and until the community understands that the incarcerated population is them—they're fathers and mothers and sisters and aunts and uncles—then those who are coming out have to overcome the prejudice, the stigma, in addition to all the other handicaps they face."

By the time of the pandemic, 30-odd classes were involved, and the organization had reached about 2,000 students total. When COVID-19 hit, the prisons went on lockdown, and part of Klarreich's mission turned to advocating for the men and women on the inside and drawing attention to their plight. "What happened inside the prisons was criminal, what [this country] did [to] incarcerated people during this period," she says. "They couldn't see their families—forget about us, no families. They had no programs—no chapel, no library, no education."

To tackle such complicated dynamics, Klarreich put her 25 years of journalism experience to work navigating the details to try to make her case to a larger audience. Her approach centered on a number of key concepts:

RELATIONSHIPS "For our access, a lot depends on the warden of the individual prison," she notes. "When the pandemic hit and we couldn't get inside, we immediately shifted to the best thing we could do, which was to get soap and hand sanitizer to our students. We were able to get ten thousand bars of soap and distributed them to various institutions. NPR wanted to do a story on this whole initiative to address what was happening in the prisons, and the prison said no."

PERSONAL CONFIDENTIALITY When Klarreich pitches journalists, she says reporters are most interested in a student's background, how they came to the program, and what it's like to be writing from the inside. "I can't think of a single media outlet that has not asked us about the crimes." For her part, she notes, "We never ask about our students' crimes. And of course, every journalist wants to ask that question. I always leave it up to the student to decide what he or she wants to reveal. The reporter can talk to the person themself; they can ask them directly if they want to know. Florida is a state where you can look up anybody for anything. They can just go on the website and see the person and say whatever they want to about their time. But that won't come from us."

ALTERNATIVE OPTIONS When you can't get a reporter to cover a situation, one solution is to write the story yourself and submit it as an op-ed column, she says. "The Department of Corrections pays attention to it, you know state legislators might. It adds a little bit of credibility to what we're doing, for sure, and then you can try to use it as leverage."

As a former reporter, Klarreich admits that moving to the other side of the microphone wasn't a lot of fun. "It was horrible," she says with a laugh. "You have to actually answer questions instead of ask them! And then also not knowing what the person's going to do with it. But obviously, because I'm passionate about the work and the results and why it's so important, I can talk a lot about it."

– 7 –

THE ART OF THE INTERVIEW

Smithville ────────────────────

Diego Lopez, the owner of Smithville Hardware and Mercantile, has not been having a very good year. A new megastore opened on the highway and has begun pulling business away from his downtown store. He hasn't had to lay anyone off yet, but he might if the numbers don't start improving. Out of the blue, he gets a call from a reporter with the local TV station. The reporter is working on a story about small businesses and how they're doing in the current economy. He'd like to come by that afternoon to talk to Diego—who has never done any media interviews before and is rather nervous about what this would involve.

Without an interview, most reporters don't have a story. They need to talk to someone to get information, quotes, sound bites, and video clips that let them create a narrative for their readers, viewers, and listeners.

Conducting an interview is fairly easy, in the grand scheme of things. Reporters who don't know a single thing about a subject can stick to the basics (that would be the who, what, when, where, why, how, and so what?) and come away with a decent amount of information.

But being interviewed is much tougher. The prospect of being on the other side of the camera or microphone or on the other end of the telephone line has been known to make the toughest people's knees turn to jelly. Worries abound: What if I forget what to say? What if I stutter? What if they ask a question I can't answer? What if my shirt has a stain on it?

You may luck out and have a great interviewer who works to set you at ease, establish a rapport, and clearly explains what they're looking for. Or you might get someone who is inexperienced, unprofessional, aggressive, or in a rush and fails to do any of those things. Unless you have established positive, constructive relationships with your local media, you don't really know what kind of a reporter you're going to get until they show up.

This chapter gives concrete advice that will help those concerns vanish, including where to look for interviewees, how to remember key points and handle tough questions, and what you should have in your interview kit.

Controlling the Interview

It's commonly believed that the interviewer, the person asking questions, is the one in control of the interview. In fact, an interview is a two-way street. Both the person asking questions and the person answering them are equally in control. You're giving them time and space to have their questions answered; it's up to you how you provide those answers. They control the questions, and that's all.

Don't tell my reporter friends this—but doing an interview isn't solely about answering their questions. It's also about telling the story that you want to tell.

Don't sweat. Stay calm. Relax.

You're in control.

Finding Spokespeople

Identifying the right person to represent your organization or company is critical. Often this will be the highest-ranking person, like the owner, CEO, or school principal. In theory, that person knows the most about your mission and the story and is experienced in handling tough situations.

But the leader isn't *always* the best spokesperson. PR practitioners across the country collectively shuddered during the BP oil spill in the Gulf of Mexico in 2010, when company CEO Tony Hayward told the media: "The first thing to say is I'm sorry. We're sorry for the massive disruption it's caused their lives. There's no one who wants this over more than I do. I'd like my life back." That last comment stoked a wave of anger against Hayward personally and against BP—especially considering that 11 people died in the explosion.

If the big boss isn't the best choice, it's time to get creative. Think beyond the traditional confines of the interviewee box. Here are a few success stories to get you started.

"Don't be afraid to look outside of the usual suspects," says brewery communications expert Justin Williams. "Find the natural storyteller in the org, someone who is curious and comfortable."

"I try to go with people who fit the demographic of the event I'm trying to promote," says marketer Adam Horwitz. "If it's a breast cancer charity that we're promoting, I'd likely try to find an employee who had breast cancer."

But that doesn't mean you just pluck Jane Smith from your social worker team and stick her in front of a camera. Jeremy Tucker, who works with an electric utility, says former members of the media can sometimes be highly effective spokespeople, because they've worked it from the opposite side of the microphone. Above all, he advises, "Spokespeople should be among the best-informed individuals at a company and have a broad understanding of all areas of the enterprise."

It's important to remember that authority within an organization does not equate to authority or trust in the public's mind. The nonprofit

Center for Food Integrity has conducted significant research into consumer trust issues—in part to figure out who the most reliable and trusted sources of information are to speak about key food topics. The character type deemed the most trusted was dubbed the "Mom Scientist," described as "a mother with scientific educational and/or work experience." You may need to go beyond the C-suite or the nonprofit's vice presidents to find the best person to represent your organization or business on a particular issue.

Practice, Practice, Practice

This can't be emphasized enough.

If you are going in front of a camera or sitting down with a newspaper writer, radio host, or podcaster, you need to practice, prepare, rehearse, record yourself, play it back, and then do it all over again.

And again.

Your statements on camera or mic should sound natural and unrehearsed—but they should never be off-the-cuff or not thought out.

That sounds confusing, and it is. Sounding natural in an interview does not come naturally to most people. We don't usually speak like we want to sound: We use verbal crutches, those ums and ahs, and our sentences ramble only to cut off mid-thought as we jump from idea to idea.

"They should practice and have a good idea of the message they want to get across beforehand, feel confident in it, and then practice some more," says Ben Nagy, a former newspaper editor who now handles communications for a labor union. Above all, he cautions, "'Winging it is not the same thing as being authentic."

Back when I was working for the state agriculture department, we were facing a potential outbreak of bird flu and I wanted to be ready with a crisis communications plan. I developed my messaging, memorized as much as I could cram into my brain, and then had my team to sit down in a conference room to play reporters. I told them to throw every random and aggressive question at me that they could think of—no topic was off-limits. They went after me mercilessly for about 30 minutes and recorded the whole thing. Yes, I cringed to hear myself stumble and trip when I played it back—but then we were able to use that back-and-forth to refine my answers and prepare even more.

Rachel Swick Mavity says that her former hospital didn't provide scripts for doctors being interviewed, but it did work with them in advance to prepare. "We only work with authentic voices," she says. "Often our doctors are incredibly familiar with the topic they will be discussing," and don't need any help in that regard.

What the staff *does* provide is practice asking and answering questions, which can help get a rhythm down for someone who hasn't been interviewed before—or tips on how to shift the topic away from questions they don't know how to handle.

Bridging Statements

The go-to technique for gracefully shifting topics is the *bridging statement*, an incredibly helpful way of redirecting the conversation in a way that allows you to answer the question that you wish you'd been asked. You *bridge* from one topic to another, moving back to the points you want to get across or pulling the conversation to topics you want to discuss. Bridging statements help you stick to your messages and keep you in control of the interview. You deliver them as you would say anything else in an interview—in a calm, controlled, natural manner.

Useful bridging statements include:

- "What's really important to remember is . . ."
- "What not many people know/understand is that . . ."
- "What I really need to emphasize here is . . ."
- "It's often surprising for people to realize that . . ."
- "The situation really boils down to . . ."
- "Looking at the big picture . . ."
- "We certainly hear people saying that, but it's just as critical to know . . ."
- "It's quite important to keep in mind that . . ."

Hundreds of other phrases and techniques can help you with your bridging; these are just a few that have worked for me. Searching online for "bridging statements" will bring up a host of others that you may find fit your manner and way of speaking better.

Bridging statements can often come in handy when asked a question that you can't or don't want to answer—without having to say "no comment."

Don't Say It

You never, ever want to say "no comment."

That might seem counterintuitive to anyone who watches a lot of political or crime dramas—don't actors playing politicians and lawyers invoke that phrase all the time?

Well, yes . . . but usually only the ones playing bad guys! In reality, "no comment" drives home the completely wrong message that you have something to hide. It suggests that anything you *could* say in response would hurt you. More importantly, "no comment" has entered popular culture to the point that it's uttered only by crooks and scandal-swept politicians.

Don't say it. Ever.

Of course, there are many excellent reasons why you might not want to speak about an issue. There may be legal issues, personnel reasons, medical issues, or other confidential topics that you would rather not get into. Or, you might want to avoid getting drawn into commenting on a contentious community or industry issue.

Thankfully, there are many other ways to deflect and decline to speak about an issue without using the phrase "no comment":

> **IF THE ISSUE IS TIMING:** "I can't get into that right now, but I'd be happy to talk about that at the appropriate time."

> **IF THE ISSUE IS NOT IN YOUR WHEELHOUSE:** "That's not an area we really work with, but I can tell you that . . ." followed by a general, safe statement.

IF YOU CAN'T TALK ABOUT IT AT ALL: "That's not something I'm at liberty to discuss."

If possible, it's always best to try to bridge to another topic, as outlined above.

"I Don't Know" Is OK

I've helped many interviewees who were initially nervous because they felt like they needed to have all the answers. They feared being made to look uninformed or incompetent on camera. The simple fact is no one can answer every question that a reporter might ask—and reporters don't expect you to, either. As long as you can address the core topic of the interview, you should be fine.

Here's what to do if your brain isn't holding the information you need, according to Jeremy Tucker: "If you don't know the answer to a question, simply say so, and call the reporter back once you have an answer."

Simple enough, right?

The trick is that you need to follow up—a call or email is fine—and make sure you send the information they need or point them in the right direction. That might be giving them the name or contact details of the person who does know, setting up an additional interview, or emailing a web link to an authoritative, reputable source.

My go-to line is usually delivered with a chuckle and a self-deprecating shake of the head: "I don't know the answer to that, but I'll check and get that information to you." Other options include "I don't have that information right at my fingertips," "I'm not the best person to talk to about that topic," or "I don't want to give you the wrong information, so let me just verify a few things and get back to you."

Reporters will understand. As a journalist, I actually liked people who told me they didn't know the answer instead of feeding me a line of made-up balderdash. I appreciated the fact that they knew what they didn't know and took the time to do the courteous, professional thing and follow up. Sometimes when they pointed me to another person, that second interview ended up providing some great perspective.

Smithville

IN ACTION: *Diego thinks that this TV interview could help draw some attention to his business, but he wants some time to plan out what he's going to say. He schedules the interview for tomorrow morning and asks for some more details about the reporter's story. He learns that there's a new report out from a national group saying that the failure rate for small businesses is growing and that many are citing competition from big chains and superstores. Armed with that information, Diego takes some time to write out and practice his main points. He also has his staff spend a little extra time cleaning and straightening the shelves in front of the cash registers, which will make a good backdrop. He moves some of his wrenches—a big sale item this month—to a shelf next to where he'll be standing, for use as a prop. At home that evening, he practices with his teenage daughter holding her cell phone and recording him and watches the playback to improve.*

Enjoy the Silence

Silence makes a lot of people uncomfortable. We try to fill it however we can—with jokes or stories, or by providing information or saying things that we shouldn't.

Reporters love silence and will try to use it to their advantage. They'll ask a question and then just—be quiet.

You'll answer.

They'll stay quiet.

You'll stare at them awkwardly.

They'll stare back at you. Quietly, of course.

Then you'll crack—anything to end the silence!—and start talking again.

Don't let that happen to you. Silence is your friend as much as it is the interviewer's. Remember that you are in control of the interview too. They're hoping you'll keep on talking to banish the quiet. Don't give in to that temptation.

Just stare back and smile until they realize you're not cracking like an egg, and they'll move on to the next question.

This is harder than it sounds. It's a known scientific fact that time expands when you're being interviewed. When you're being quizzed on camera, what seems like 15 minutes is probably more like five. So those 30 seconds of silence may feel like a few minutes. Don't give in—just wait them out.

Assemble Your Interview Kit

You never know when a reporter is going to come calling, or when you'll be called upon to speak to the press. Someone might reach out at the end of the day, while you're on vacation, or after you just finished mucking out the cow barn. An experienced interviewee will have a kit containing all the personal and professional items needed to handle a last-minute request. Here's what my kit contained, plus a few items that may come in handy depending on your situation. These are mostly for in-person or on-camera interviews; telephone interviews have a different dynamic and will be covered later.

☐ A change of clothes, or at least a clean shirt and tie or blouse and blazer. The blazer gives you an extra boost of professionalism and also hides sweat and ketchup stains from lunch. Alternatively, a nice polo shirt with your organization's logo or name will suffice in 90 percent of situations.

☐ For people who shave, an extra razor to get rid of that pesky one o'clock shadow.

- [ ] A pack of gum or mints for a quick breath-freshener. (But please don't chew gum during the interview.)

- [ ] A pair of sensible, sturdy shoes, in case the reporter needs to do a tour or talk to you while you're walking.

- [ ] A copy of any talking points you might need.

- [ ] A copy of the news release or other information related to this interview, so you can give it to the reporter at the end of the interview.

- [ ] A business card, if you have one. If not, make sure your contact information is featured prominently on the news release.

- [ ] A comb or brush and hairspray—plus anything else you need to convince your hair to cooperate. You don't want the audience distracted by the aftermath of your afternoon bedhead.

- [ ] Makeup. Keep it subtle. If you never wear makeup in real life, you might still want a little powder to make the camera like you better and avoid shiny skin.

- [ ] Nail trimmers. Your hands may get a close-up or be in the shot, so do a quick check to make sure your fingernails are looking good.

- [ ] Contact lenses. If you wear contacts, use them in the interview. This avoids any odd glare off your glasses lenses.

- [ ] A silenced cell phone. The last thing you want during an interview is the distraction of your cell phone ringing with a call, beeping with a text, or quacking with an alarm.

- [ ] If relevant, a fresh mask in line with the current company protocols or local regulations.

Date, Time, Location

Just like when you're planning events (see Chapter 8), preparing for an interview centers around the date, time, and location. The date part of that formula is self-explanatory. As for the time, you need to have a good sense of not just when the interview begins, but how long you can expect it to last. (You may expect 15 minutes, say, when the reporter knows they'll need 30. Get on the same page to start.) A good practice is to add 15 minutes to the interviewer's estimate. That gives both of you some extra flex time in case questions or answers run over, or if you need to look something up at the end.

The location is the part that needs some advance planning. Ask yourself and the reporter such questions as: Are they coming to you, or are you going to them? If it'll be an outdoor interview, what's the weather forecast—and what's your backup plan in case that forecast is woefully wrong? If your workspace isn't the best—a tiny office maybe or a dangerous construction site—can you meet at a neutral location, like a park or library? Will they want a tour of your facilities first, and what's the best route for that? If you're going to a TV studio for an interview on set, what are the seating arrangements like? Work through every option and have a backup plan. You may find that you have to split things up to get the right combination of good visuals and a great interview.

For example, let's say you're the general manager of a construction company specializing in roads and bridges. You just put out a story about your 75th anniversary celebration, and a reporter wants to interview you on a jobsite. The problem is that the site today is far too noisy, with heavy machinery moving around and traffic whizzing by on the nearby interstate. Your compromise is to do the interview outdoors at a city park a few miles away and then take the reporter on a tour of the site to get B-roll footage. Problem solved, and their story just got better.

For a phone interview, verify who's calling whom. That avoids the awkward dance where both people are sitting, staring at their phones, waiting for the other to call first. Try to get a backup phone number if possible; cell phones have been known to conk out or lose reception.

Remote Interviews

If I had been writing this chapter in the fall of 2019, a section on remote video interviews wouldn't have existed. Overnight, the COVID-19 pandemic transformed the way reporting was done, bringing remote interviews into the mainstream of local television news and enhancing newspapers' abilities to do video interviews without wasting a videographer's valuable time. Doing a video interview suddenly became the norm rather than the exception. Even though COVID-19 restrictions have relaxed, many media outlets are using video interviews in at least some cases because of the convenience and ease of scheduling. Make sure you clarify who's hosting and sending the link and get a phone number you can call in case of technical difficulties. Log on or test it in advance to familiarize yourself with the system. Check yourself on your webcam before joining the call, to make sure your hair isn't standing on end, the sun's not blazing straight into the camera, and so forth.

Owing to their technical needs, television stations may have their own quirks. When I logged on to Zoom for a video interview with a local station about a previous book I'd written, I was surprised to find myself talking to a black screen. I couldn't see the interviewer, but he could see me. It was slightly jarring and threw me off a little bit—but I quickly got over it and the interview went well. Ask in advance what you're going to see and hear and if there's anything special you need to know.

What to Wear

One of the most common questions I'm asked when helping people prepare for broadcast or video interviews is: "What should I wear?" Television is a visual medium, and even people without prior media experience know that how you look makes a huge difference in how you and your messages are perceived.

I'm not a fashion expert by any stretch of the imagination, but I do know the basics for an on-camera conversation:

> Solid colors always beat out stripes or patterns. Some patterns will make your shirt or jacket look like it's crawling across the screen. (This goes for ties, as well. Skip that favorite tiny-pattern necktie and go with a single color.)

> Never, ever wear green, or anything with green in it. If green screen technology is used, your torso or parts of it can blend into the background, leading to a rather disconcerting disembodied head-and-arms look.

> For dress shirts and blouses, blue beats plain white. Avoid black clothing too.

> Wear no jewelry, or minimize it. Aside from the jangly noise factor, it can be a distraction for viewers.

Working with Newspaper Reporters

We established earlier, in Chapter 5, that newspaper reporters generally ask the deepest and most penetrating questions. They are typically seeking a level of depth and detail that broadcast rarely has time for.

Newspaper and online journalists are often on the hunt for information that explains the meaning behind the news rather than just imparting the facts. That means they're looking for quotes that encapsulate a complicated issue, or a real-life story that elaborates on a key point. Some reporters will come at a story with a narrative already sketched out in their heads; it's up to you to correct any problems or inaccuracies in those assumptions.

To plan for a newspaper interview in particular, take as much time as you can to anticipate their questions and figure out your answers. Questions can flow on from each prior question; if you go down one path, take that line of questioning to its logical conclusion and think about how to address each point you want to make. A half-hour newspaper interview can cover a lot of ground, so prepare as much as you can.

Ten Rules of Thumb to Remember

Here are ten best practices for a range of interview questions or situations:

1. **HIT THE FIRST PITCH OVER THE FENCE.** An interview will often start with a general question for background, along the lines of "So tell me about . . ." This is the best type of question to be asked, completely open-ended. In baseball terms, it's just hanging there waiting for you to hit it out of the park. It's a chance to frame the topic in your terms, provide important information, and supply your context.

2. **ANSWER QUESTIONS; DON'T RESPOND TO STATEMENTS.** Especially in broadcast media, interviewers often don't ask too many questions. Instead, they'll make a statement, pause, and wait for you to agree, disagree, or respond somehow. You don't have to answer questions that haven't been asked. Just wait them out or ask (politely but firmly), "What's the question?"

3. **BEWARE OF THE "SOME PEOPLE SAY" GAME.** Reporters sometimes frame a point this way to get you to respond to some criticism or attacks from an unknown individual. In some cases, the reporter hasn't actually talked to anyone saying that—they just know someone is saying it, possibly on a national level. You don't need to get drawn into responding to anonymous or unknown people. It may suit your purposes to respond to that type of a question if you're seeking to refute a particular criticism—but it might not. Feel free to ask point-blank who's saying that; if they can't name anyone, you can (again, politely) decline to respond to hypothetical statements or anonymous critics.

4. **LOOK OUT FOR TOUGH QUESTIONS HIDING IN PLAIN SIGHT.** Some reporters, particularly of the investigative variety,

may come to you just seeking one particular piece of information. They may ask you a barrage of softer questions to get you in the swing of answering freely and openly, toss their main question in the middle, and then swiftly move on to more of the easy questions. You might not even realize that was their play until you see the resulting article in print. Listen carefully to what's being asked and take your time with each answer. (This is also a great reminder to follow the advice in Chapter 5 about doing your research on reporters and editors, so you know who's who when they contact you.)

5. **PUT THINGS INTO PERSPECTIVE.** What a reporter needs most from an interview—the secret sauce that transforms their story from pedestrian to truly great—is often context, rather than pure information. Some reporters may not consciously think about or ask for it, but you can provide that value anyway. Just add some context to every answer, like this:

QUESTION: How big is this problem?

ANSWER: Sarah, we need to remember that 2 out of 10 people in Smithville County are living with diabetes. That's why our new nutrition campaign is so important to improving their health and lives.

QUESTION: What's new with the library these days?

ANSWER: Thanks for asking that, Binh. We want to expand the library's services by being open seven days a week and buying more books for young adult readers. But if the upcoming ballot measure fails, we will have to make cuts and eliminate popular programs like our kids' summer reading club. That will affect 600young people right here in Smithville.

QUESTION: What programs do you have at Smithville Vo-Tech High School?

ANSWER: We offer 16 programs to prepare our youth for their future careers, ranging from cosmetology to carpentry. Our most popular program is Health Careers—over 100 students each year earn their Certified Nurse Assistant (CNA) certifications while still in school. What's important to know is that we also have programs in the area middle schools to get students thinking about these options early, and we're looking to expand that next year to double the number of middle-schoolers reached.

6. **USE BODY LANGUAGE TO YOUR ADVANTAGE.** The signals that your body sends in an interview can help guide a reporter just as much as your words do. Use that to help you get your messages across. When you're making an especially important point, lean forward. To punctuate a sentence, use a natural hand gesture. Smile to help set them at ease and build a personal connection. If they're asking a question that you like or is particularly good, nod along as they speak.

7. **AVOID CROSSTALK AND INTERRUPTIONS.** It's human nature to want to rush into a conversation and start talking even before the questioner is done. In an interview, you want to avoid this for several reasons. First, particularly in a broadcast interview, it reduces the chances that your quotes can be neatly edited into the final story, as they'll be mixed up with the interviewer's voice and hard to hear. Second, you should make sure you understand the complete question before answering; you may think you know what's being asked but perhaps not. And third, even a brief pause will give you a few seconds more to gather your thoughts and provide the clearest answers. Just wait until the interviewer is done with their question before you jump in. You can still show enthusiasm

with your tone of voice and by using body language strategically, as described above.

8. **IF POSSIBLE, OFFER ADVICE.** One of my favorite questions to ask an expert is "What advice would you give to someone in X situation?" That could be advice to someone getting started in their professional field, advice to a person experiencing something relating to their area of expertise, or advice on how to navigate a certain situation that they can speak to. This is another way of humanizing a highly technical or complicated issue and providing additional context and perspective. Don't be afraid to offer advice on your own, without being asked or prompted.

9. **BE TRUTHFUL.** Always be honest. Never tell a lie. Never shade the truth. This should go without saying, but it deserves repeating. Don't exaggerate, stretch the story, or mischaracterize your expertise. You'll get in more trouble by attempting to deceive than by simply being straightforward and transparent. Remember, it's OK to say that you don't know.

10. **KEEP YOUR COOL.** Always stay calm. Breathe steadily and evenly. Video viewers will remember the redness of your face and the beads of sweat popping out on your forehead far more than they'll remember your words. Radio listeners will pick up on any tension in your voice and the tone of your answers very easily, and be able to tell if you're rattled.

Smithville

IN ACTION: The day of the interview is here at last. Diego puts on a light-blue store polo shirt with his logo prominently on the chest. (He also brings a backup shirt in case he spills coffee on the first one.) He's confident in what he wants to say and knows not to say "no comment" if there's a question he doesn't want to answer. When the reporter arrives and sets up his camera, Diego positions himself so that both the shelf of tools and equipment and his cash registers are in the background. To emphasize a point about personal service, he picks up a wrench while telling a story about recently helping a local handyman get the right tool for his business. The reporter loves his style and approach. The hardest question he asks is whether Diego hates big-box chain stores, but Diego's ready with a smile and a soft answer that bridges back to his main points about the importance of shopping locally: "We love competition, but a giant corporate chain doesn't know the community and can't offer the same service like we can."

Simplifying a Complicated Topic

If you work with any sort of complex issue, technical material, or sophisticated business details, chances are that your average reporter isn't going to understand half of what you're saying if you're not careful. You need to come prepared for an interview with simple analogies, stories, or phrases that can cut to the heart of your subject. If you spend any time on the social media site Reddit, you may be familiar with the concept of ELI5—Explain Like I'm 5. That's a good exercise to do for these kinds of topics. Break it down into its simplest terms and explain it to a family member or coworker who's not familiar with the subject in as intimate terms as you are. If they're still confused or have questions, hone it down even more.

When I was working for the state department of agriculture, I had to manage a lot of misconceptions about farms today, including the incorrect idea that they're mainly run by large multinational corporations. In my state, more than 90 percent of farms are family owned and operated. I quickly stopped using terms commonly used by farmers themselves—phrases like "agribusiness operations" and "growers"—and used the simple words "family farms" everywhere I could. That helped reporters understand that buying local goods really has an impact on families in our area, and the money doesn't flow to faceless multinational corporations.

Repeating Yourself

One of my fears when I do an interview is that I'll run out of things to say and just start repeating myself. That can be solved by preparing solid talking points and reviewing them frequently before the interview.

That said, there are legitimate situations where you intentionally have to repeat the same line—such as not being able to discuss details of an ongoing investigation, or because something is a personnel matter. You may *want* to respond, but for whatever reason, you simply can't.

A tenacious reporter who really wants an answer will keep asking their question in different ways to try to get some sort of a usable quote or admission or information. In those cases, you have to stick to your statement, stay calm and collected, and just repeat it again as needed. Don't go off-script. The best approach for handling an aggressive reporter is to simply state your reply over and over.

A former spokesman for a state governor that I worked with called this technique "The [Tough Reporter] Answer," using the example of a particularly dogged local journalist who was known for asking the same question 20 different ways. That reporter has their job to do, and you have yours. Stick to your answer and don't try to start speaking off the cuff. Eventually they'll stop asking. You may take a little heat, but getting pressure from a reporter is better than having to explain to your organization's attorney why you disclosed confidential information.

Talking Points

A few times now we've referred to talking points, also called speaking points. In their purest form, your talking points are simply a list of items that you want to talk about. They're usually written in a bullet-point list for ease of reference. You can map them out in outline form, use single words to jog your memory, or write down phrases or partial sentences to make sure you use the right words. If you're preparing talking points for someone else, find out how they want them presented. Unless you're on a phone call, you typically won't be able to refer back to them during an interview, so they're primarily to help you prepare and memorize your key topics.

Don't overthink them; they're just another tool in your toolbox.

Off and On the Record

In journalism, there are a host of different ways you can be quoted or cited: On the record, off the record, on background, on deep background, not for attribution . . . the list goes on.

You're better off not worrying about any of that. Just stick to the two basics: on the record, where everything you say can be used, and off the record, where nothing you say can be quoted or reported.

Unless there are very delicate circumstances requiring you to explain a sensitive situation that can't be reported, you're far better with just keeping everything on the record.

Always remember: A reporter has to agree to put something off the record, and they usually don't want to do that. You can't unilaterally declare that you're going off, and you can't put something off the record after you've already said it *on* the record.

Acing the Radio Interview

Radio people are sticklers for audio quality, because without clear, crisp sound, they don't have a story. They like to have their interviewees in front of them in the studio sitting on the other side of the microphone for the best sound. Still, the majority of radio interviews these days will be over the phone. Whenever possible, call in on a landline, as that offers the highest quality. If you have to call on a cell phone, dial in a few minutes in advance to test out various locations in your home or office. (I once did an interview from my closet because it had the best audio quality. I had no idea that pants and shirts improved the sound!). Make sure your battery is charged just in case the call goes long.

If you're in your office, shut the door and put a sign on it to avoid interruptions. Never do an interview in public or outdoors—there's too much ambient noise that will mess with the quality. If you have to, get in your car and find an empty corner of a parking lot.

Do you hate the sound of your voice on a recording? Many people do. Despite that, if you have the time in advance, record yourself running through your talking points, and then play it back. You'll pick up on problems with speed, tone, and clarity that you can correct and adjust before you get on the air.

And remember that there's nothing wrong with having your talking points in front of you, on a computer screen or printed out. I often use this little cheat to guide me along, make sure I don't forget anything, and guarantee that I touch on all the points I want to make.

For interviews that will be recorded, edited, and broadcast later, you need to focus on creating clear, concise quotes that can be clipped and edited into a story. Talk at a nice, steady cadence, and speak as precisely as possible. Avoid crosstalk (as noted above), and take a pause before you start a new idea.

For live interviews, such as a call-in talk show, you'll typically be given a time slot of 5 or 10 minutes. Live radio is the most nerve-racking to me, because you can't get a do-over—but it's actually fairly simple to navigate. Your average talk-show host will have a handful of questions and will be relying on you to talk at length to cover those topics, so be prepared with stories, examples, and context to amplify the primary points you want to make. Remember that you're being given an open channel to thousands of listeners, so use it wisely—mention your business name and website address or phone number naturally but frequently.

If the live host needs to break in and interrupt, they'll do that. When a host comes to a hard stop, they'll signal you with a question like "In the 30 seconds we have left, can you talk about . . . ?" Make sure you hit that stop and don't run over, or you'll get cut off abruptly. I like to have an analog clock or a timer running on a stopwatch to help gauge that and end on time. Throw in a cheerful "Thanks for having me" at the end, and you'll be good.

THE TAKEAWAY

Interviews can be terrifying, even for people who've been working around the media for years. Just remember that you're just as much in control of the interview as the reporter is.

Prepare and plan ahead by doing these five things:

- Find the right person to speak for your company.
- Practice, then practice some more. Then go back and practice again.
- Don't say "no comment"; instead, use language that lets you bridge to another topic.
- Build an interview kit so you have a clean shirt and nice hair.
- Never go off the record.

Above all, stay cool and collected. The reporter doesn't have much of a story without you.

"If I were a reporter, what would I ask?"

Like that of many people working in public relations, Amy Higgins's path to PR was through journalism. She worked in trade publications—such as those we discussed in Chapter 5—for about a decade, writing and editing for magazines covering the metal, automotive, recreational, and machinery industries. When she moved to managing communications for the Elyria City School District, outside Cleveland, Ohio, she brought many of the same skills.

"The industries that I was in were very technical, and my degree is in communications, so I wasn't an engineer," Higgins recalls. "It taught me how to talk to people and how to relate to people that I had nothing in common with—and how to simplify information so that it would make sense to anyone who was reading it."

Those skills and that experience are also useful when doing interviews with the media. Acing an interview is largely about planning, Higgins says. Here's her top advice for getting ready for an interview whether she's preparing herself or prepping another staff member or expert for an interview:

Anticipate in advance: "I try to anticipate what they might want to know. I think about it beforehand—'If I were a reporter, what would I ask?' I try to make little notes and think about if it goes down a certain path, what would my answer be?"

Lean on specialists: "I'm clearly not an expert, I'm not an educator. . . . I learn stuff through osmosis over the years. I do rely on our experts for things a reporter wants to know—if there's a new House bill and how does it impact us, if there are funding implications, how is that going to affect the budget. . . . Is it the operations director, is it a teacher."

Do a pre-interview: "I try to get information from the reporter beforehand—'What kinds of topics are you looking to cover, what do you really want to focus on.' Kind of a preinterview with them to help me understand what they're really looking for to decide who the best person is to address that."

Follow up: "Occasionally they ask something that's unexpected. But I've always found if that happens to me in an interview, I'm just honest, and say that I'm going to get back to you. 'I'm not positive where we are with that, I'll get back to you.' And then get back to them—don't leave them hanging."

Doing an on-camera interview with a TV reporter may strike fear into the hearts of many people—not so for Higgins. One of her favorite times to do a TV interview, she says, is during a crisis (see more in Chapter 9). "It's one of the few times when you truly get to tell your story without any filter whatsoever," she says. "Those on-the-spot live interviews are a great thing, to me, because we get to tell our story directly and powerfully." And that, in turn, stems from the relationships she's built with her local media: "They knew that if they called and needed a quick on-camera interview, I'd be willing to do it, and they appreciate that."

− 8 −

THE SCIENCE OF
EVENTS

Smithville ────────────────────────────────

*Erica Olson is in her third year as camp director at Mount
Smithville Summer Camp, a sleepover program for kids aged 8
to 15. She wants to help boost attendance this summer from kids
whose parents haven't thought about summer camp before, and
thinks media coverage could help build awareness. She wants
to take advantage of some good weather in mid-March to pull
together a media event showcasing the camp's new programs—
blacksmithing, stand-up paddle-boarding, and climbing and rap-
pelling down its 60-foot climbing tower.*

Holding an event is easy, right? Just get people, a purpose, and
an activity or reason for being there. When you're holding an
event for the express purpose of getting media attention, however, the
dynamic shifts, and there are a lot more details that you need to be
aware of. This chapter is your guide to media events.

Is This Event Necessary?

I've worked for people who wanted a media event practically every
week, and for people who couldn't have cared less about public speaking or the press. Your leadership's experiences, your organization's
strategic goals, and leaders' individual preferences will go a long way

toward creating an outline for your media event strategy. But the important thing is that events should be strategic and well planned, not pulled out of a hat at the last minute. You want an event to have a clear purpose and direction for everything from the speakers' list to the timing. You don't want to step on or compete with other events, or become known for wasting the media's time with announcements that have little news value.

I'm a strong believer in the less-is-more principle. If you save your media events for your biggest news, the media will recognize that and show up. By contrast, if you're crying wolf and issuing breathless advisories that don't truly rise to the level of real news, the media's going to stop turning out, and your organization's reputation is going to suffer. You shouldn't hold an event just to burnish someone's ego. Start your planning by asking the fundamental question of whether you even need a media event. Some stories are best told through a news release and follow-up interviews, not a full-on press conference with lectern and backdrops.

Stay Organized

Whether you have a month or a week to plan and execute your event, staying organized is essential. Keep a master document that members of your team can refer to with the latest details—Google Docs or another shared cloud service is perfect for this. It should include at a minimum:

- background information on the context and event
- the four or five specific messaging points that your event will be emphasizing
- an agenda for the event, including order of speakers and who will introduce them
- contact information for all the speakers and other VIPs invited
- assignments and a timeline—who's doing what and when

VIPs Aren't Always a Draw

Many people outside of politics think that the very presence of a Very Important Person will have the press enthralled, or at least interested. Sometimes a VIP can, indeed, be a huge draw if they're someone the press doesn't see all the time. For example, California is the most populous state, with almost 40 million people. Getting one of the state's two US senators to attend your event would be huge. In Delaware, which has about 1 million people total, people see their federal elected officials in line at the grocery store, so it's not as big a draw. Reporters also talk with elected VIPs more than the average citizen, so they're not starstruck by having a member of Congress or your state attorney general there.

What elected officials *can* give you is credibility, especially if you're trying something new or particularly innovative. If they're endorsing your nonprofit's campaign and sharing a personal story or announcing a piece of legislation that complements your news, then that's something you should tell the press in advance so they understand that connection.

You ideally want to have elected officials speaking who have a relationship with what you're doing. State Senator Random talking about the benefits of a school project is so-so, but if you can get the chairperson of the Senate Education Committee there, that's a plus.

Care and Feeding of Elected Officials

If you do have an elected official at your event, be aware that they often require very specific handling. Especially at the statewide level, "electeds" expect a certain degree of deference and acknowledgment of their authority. Here are some key items to take into consideration when working with elected officials:

> **INVITE THEM IN ADVANCE** Don't wait until the last minute to ask. Get on their calendar as early as possible. If you really, really want a particular person there, you'll probably have to work

your event around their schedule. In my experience, elected officials' staff often don't confirm events until three or four weeks out—and even after that, they may cancel or reschedule based on the vagaries of politics, government, and personalities. They may require you to fill out an online invitation form first, which helps their staff decide which events to attend. Provide as much detail as you can about the event, who else will be attending or has been invited, and what exactly will happen.

DON'T BLINDSIDE THEM Make the invitee's role in the event crystal clear. In your invitation, specify whether they'll have a speaking role, or just be there for support. It's perfectly fine to say that speaking is up to them, but you'll need to check back closer to the date to confirm.

BE PREPARED FOR CHANGES Even if a particular person has said they don't want to speak, be ready for them to change their mind at the last minute, or to just to step up to the lectern for brief, impromptu remarks. Also expect last-minute dropouts; don't build your entire event around any one person's presence.

GET NAMES AND TITLES RIGHT Verify pronunciations and proper titles well in advance of the event. Even if the invitee is just there for moral support and a photo op, make sure that a senior person at least mentions their name and position during the event.

CHECK THE DETAILS Make sure you have their political party noted for your own reference. Research whether any legislators or council members are feuding, and don't seat them together. Ensure that if you're thanking one person for sponsoring a bill, you also thank any cosponsors who are present.

CONSIDER A VIDEO MESSAGE You may find that a particular official just can't make your event. If that's the case, ask them to record a video message to be played there, either welcoming attendees to the event or addressing one of your key message points. VIPs like this because it's highly efficient for them. An elected official can record 10 short videos to address 10 different organizations in a single hour.

Protocol and Propriety

When you're dealing with elected-official VIPs—at a media event or otherwise—there are certain niceties that must be observed to ensure that you're offering the proper respect and deference to their roles.

First, double-check the pronunciation of their names. Listen to local news or check with their staff if you're not absolutely sure. The last thing you want is for your executive director to mispronounce the name of the person she is introducing. This applies to everyone, of course, but especially to elected officials, who will assume—rightly or wrongly—that everyone knows who they are.

Second, use the person's title (Senator, Secretary, Governor, etc.) and last name until you're invited to use their first names. Some won't care at all and will think the use of titles is just silly, but others will definitely mind and will be offended if they aren't addressed properly.

Third, whether hosting officials at a dinner or introducing speakers at an event, you don't need to guess the order; just follow the standard protocol used by the US Department of State (see below). For seating and introductions, the order is most important to least important; for speaking, the order is least important to most important.

What exactly does that look like? For international diplomatic events, the State Department has a 15-page comprehensive document outlining the precise order, but for local events that don't involve ambassador-rank officials, this will generally suffice. (And if you're lucky enough to get any national-level players to attend your event, you'll be working at a much higher level and have federal protocol staff and advance teams to rely on.) Here is the basic national-level order for introductions and seating:

1.   President of the United States

2. Vice President of the United States
3. Governor of the state you're in
4. Speaker of the US House of Representatives
5. Chief Justice of the United States
6. Former Presidents
7. Former Vice Presidents
8. Members of the Supreme Court
9. Members of the Cabinet, in order of the date each department was established
10. Leadership of the US Senate
11. Members of the US Senate, in order of length of service
12. Governors outside their own states, in order of their state's admission to the Union
13. Leadership of the US House of Representatives
14. Members of the US House of Representatives, in order of length of service
15. Former Senators, Governors, and members of the House
16. Lieutenant Governor of the state you're in
17. Mayor of the city you're in
18. Mayors of other cities
19. State senators
20. State representatives

Trim that down, obviously, for your own circumstances; chances are excellent that you're not going to have members of the Supreme Court or former presidents on hand. My quick-and-dirty version when I was working in state government was this:

1. Governor
2. Federal officials: US Senate and US House
3. State Cabinet officials
4. President Pro Tempore of the state senate
5. Speaker of the state house
6. Members of the state senate

7. Members of the state house
8. Mayors and local council members

Remember that when determining the order of speakers at an event, the above order is reversed: Start with the bottom and work your way up. The first person to speak at a media event may be the site host or a representative of your organization who can get the audience's attention and kick things off smoothly. Depending on the circumstances and details, you might ask a local mayor or city council member to welcome the attendees, particularly when the local government doesn't have a real role in what you're announcing.

It's critically important that you coordinate talking points among the speakers. I've been at events where a state senator steals all the thunder from the later speakers—the governor and US senator who were there to do the formal announcement—leaving those dignitaries with absolutely nothing to say and forcing them to think quickly on their feet. Some politicians are good at that and can pull it off without a hitch; others are not as proficient at speaking off the cuff and will be awkward. All of them will likely be embarrassed and upset, and for good reason.

Event Hall of Shame

The worst events are the ones where nothing is happening. These include what are popularly known as "press conferences," which can be summed up as a man in a suit standing behind a lectern droning on about something. They are utterly interchangeable and completely forgettable.

The media hates these, particularly because they almost never offer the opportunity for interesting visuals. If you put one on, you've just sabotaged yourself and probably doomed your great story to run deep inside the newspaper or website rather than on page A1 or the site's homepage just because it doesn't have a photo. You might not get on the local television broadcast at all. Unfair? Maybe. But both newspapers and television are visual media, and they have to draw their readers and viewers in. You don't do that with a giant wall of text or a boring video.

Here are some prime examples of bad events, and how you can turn them into good events:

A PERSON BEHIND A LECTERN The problem with this arrangement is that it projects stiffness and stodginess. Most people, even those who are accomplished speakers, will rely heavily on their notes and probably lean on the lectern just because it's there. That doesn't create a good visual. If you have an announcement that really does not lend itself to good optics, at least hold it in an interesting location with a good backdrop. For example, your nonprofit housing agency could hold its event in a house that's being renovated, with bare 2x4s and wires in the background. Your school district could hold one in an empty classroom with student artwork on the walls.

> **IF YOU MUST:** If there's absolutely no other alternative, then after the formal announcement, offer the media one-on-one interviews so they don't have to rely on "the speech."

RIBBON-CUTTING Local chambers of commerce love to hold ribbon-cuttings for new businesses. Local newspapers hate to run those photos. What could be more tedious and fake than people grinning and stretching a ribbon while holding a giant pair of pretend scissors? If you're opening a business, don't you want the focus to be on your products or services? Take a photo in the heart of the business—in the welcoming lobby of the real estate firm, on a jobsite of the construction company, or in the aisles of the bookstore.

> **INSTEAD:** If you still want to have the ribbon-cutting celebration, be creative and inventive. Home Depot store openings have featured a large orange sign sawed down the middle. Whole Foods has broken bread straight from their bakery. Your candy shop can do a ceremonial fudge-sampling for its new location, or the high school can slice a stack of homework in half to mark its new computer lab opening.

A GIANT CHECK Foundations and other grant-makers really enjoy those giant stunt checks because they get the name of the organization front and center. But they also display a lack of originality and creativity. Instead of focusing on the money, pull together a room full of beneficiaries or clients to talk about the organization's work and your accomplishments.

> **INSTEAD:** If you want the name of the grant-maker included in the TV broadcast, place a large poster or pull-up display prominently in the background.

GROUNDBREAKING Stop right there. Don't even think about taking a photo at the start of a project with hardhat-wearing people smiling with shovels in hand. That's as stale as month-old bread. It's been played out time and time again, and editors are generally sick of running those kinds of photos—so they'll stick them as far inside the paper as possible. Even if the story is about ground being broken for a particular project, you don't have to illustrate it with that kind of image.

> **INSTEAD** If you really want to find a way to recognize the VIPs and funders and leaders involved in your project, you can still do that with a beam-signing ceremony—as Chris Eccleston did in Chapter 3—or burying a time capsule or something similar. You don't have to line them up for a "grip and grin" with shovels every single time.

Smithville

IN ACTION: Erica's boss, the camp's program director, is very enthusiastic about the media event and has assembled a team of summer staff members to talk about the new programs. She's also arranged for Smithville's mayor and a few city council members to attend and invited the director of her state's Children in Nature program to speak about the importance of outdoor recreation. Instead of holding a ribbon-cutting, she's decided to hold a ceremonial rope-tying in front of the climbing tower—a great visual—and has recruited the mayor to take the first climb.

Plan It Out, Step by Step

What you see on television and in the movies doesn't typically reflect reality. There are very few dramatic press conferences on courthouse steps these days, despite what you see in the legal dramas. Do you remember Tony Stark's impulsive reveal in the first *Iron Man* movie? "I am Iron Man," he declared from the lectern, to a roomful of gasping reporters and flashing cameras.

That's not usually what happens. A good rule of thumb is to never put someone in front of the media unless you know exactly what they're going to say! Outline the topics and do run-throughs; this is especially helpful for clients, particularly kids, who aren't accustomed to speaking in public. Share talking points to make sure that, say, your CEO isn't planning to cover the same ground as your state senator and that the school board president isn't sharing the same story as your math teacher.

Logistics Checklist

Here are the key things to ask about and keep in mind when you're arranging logistics and planning the overall event:

- [ ] **DO I NEED A SOUND SYSTEM?** Will the small outdoor event be fine with no sound amplification, or will there be a lot of traffic on the nearby highway that we'll be competing with? (When you check out your site in advance, be there the same time of day as your event will take place.) A good portable PA system is a few hundred dollars and will prove to be an excellent investment on other occasions as well.

☐ **WHAT IS THE BACKDROP GOING TO BE?** When a TV crew sets up to interview your boss, what will viewers see in the background? Make sure it's something that reinforces your message—or is neutral at least. If you're a housing organization talking about investment in run-down properties, a good background would be a teardown house with caution tape—or a sparkling new home that's the result of your previous work. Is your elementary school launching a new outdoor classroom? Set the shot up so the backdrop showcases trees and bushes, not a brick wall. Always double- and triple-check your background. You may recall the example of former Alaska Governor Sarah Palin being interviewed on camera at a farm—apparently oblivious to a series of turkeys being slaughtered behind her! That surely wasn't the image her staff wanted to project.

☐ **DO WE NEED SEATING? OR A TENT?** Having seating of some sort is always a good idea, especially if you expect children, older people, or people with disabilities to attend. If your event is more than a few minutes long or involves multiple speakers, seating is a necessity. Also important for outdoor events is some sort of cover or shelter. Pop-up canopies can be had for relatively cheap and provide shade against the hot sun or protection against rain. The last thing you want is your audience sweating in the sun or getting drenched by a downpour.

☐ **ARE WE SERVING FOOD OR DRINKS?** It's common at some events to have some sort of a nosh, like bagels or pastries in the early morning. (Note that some reporters' ethics codes bar them from eating food at events—don't push it on them.) During the heat of the summer, having bottled water is an excellent idea. You don't want anyone passing out from the heat, especially older attendees. Bring a large cooler with several icepacks and stick it at the back of the room or tent.

☐ **HOW LONG WILL THE EVENT LAST?** Make sure you have a good sense of the overall timing as well as the timing of each element of the event. A minute-by-minute tick-tock outline can be very helpful. Communicate that timeline to your partners and speakers and stick to it. VIPs are often on a tight schedule and need to attend other functions, and the media needs to know how much time to set aside as well.

☐ **WHAT'S THE BAD-WEATHER PLAN?** Even if the forecast calls for sunny skies and 75 degrees, you need to have a backup plan. The day that you don't have a plan is the day you'll need it. Look at tents and canopies to guard against a little rain, as well as nearby indoor sites that you can move people to if a storm comes in moving fast.

Other Options

We've spent a lot of time talking about "media events" in the context of a news conference because that's what many bosses or managers expect. They want to have that time to shine behind the lectern or to do the groundbreaking. And from your perspective, news conferences can be a good tool for managing large groups of reporters, or large numbers of players, partners, and funders who all need their turn in the spotlight. News conferences can be an excellent way to manage the news and get all the information out there at once.

But formal news conferences aren't your only option. In fact, if you *really* want to attract the press, they should probably be your last resort. Think creatively.

Events for Fun

Many organizations have gotten fantastic publicity through offbeat events that are less news-oriented and more feature-focused. You can end up with a wonderfully positive story by going off the beaten path and trying something truly innovative.

If you're a nonprofit or school with a fundraising arm, your development team will love it if you can work together and have a two-for-one event that generates both revenue and publicity. In Delaware, the local Special Olympics chapter does an annual "Over the Edge" fundraiser that has local celebrities and ordinary people raise money for their attempt to rappel 17 stories down the side of an office building. Sounds scary? You're right, it is—that's part of the thrill and excitement. Each participant has to raise at least $1,100 in pledges for the Special Olympics.

The nonprofit often gets local radio hosts and TV reporters in on the game, and they in turn cover the heck out of the event and promote it for many weeks in advance. Other media outlets that don't have staff participating are still drawn to the spectacle of people sliding 222 feet down the side of a high-rise tower.

If you don't do fundraisers, you can put on other events to draw attention. A local resort's chamber of commerce in my hometown routinely sponsors a sandcastle-building contest on the beach, attracting countless participants of all skill levels. Kids come out with buckets and shovels to work alongside professional sand sculptors who create masterworks. It always gets great publicity and promotes the resort as a family destination.

A bicycle shop can find a parking lot and hold a free bike safety rodeo and tune-up day. A Scout group can do a cook-off with challenging ingredients like jalapeño peppers or creme-filled doughnuts. With the right approach, event like these are almost guaranteed to get good news coverage. If you can imagine it, you can do it and get attention for it.

Smithville

IN ACTION: After reading about how other nonprofits have held similar events, Erica has reached out to local reporters and invited them to stay after the formal event and do some of the new activities themselves—writing or producing first-person accounts of what it's like to go stand-up paddle-boarding, hammer away on a blacksmith's forge, or climb up and rappel down a 60-foot wall. In her email, she included background statistics on the growth of stand-up paddle-boarding, the history of blacksmithing in Smithville County, and the intense training that sport climbers undertake, giving the reporters a taste of how they could tie it into a trend or historical retrospective. All the media outlets but one eagerly said yes, and that one asked if their reporter could come another day because of a conflict.

Annual Events

If you're an organization or business that holds an event every year that's largely the same, like a business expo, comic convention, or open house, you know that reporters eventually lose interest and stop coming. The same old thing year after year is just not news.

It's your job to find new angles to pitch to them. That often involves working directly with organizers as part of the planning process to make sure they're thinking of publicity opportunities. For example:

The local outdoors show that focuses on hunting and camping can do a simple hands-on geocaching program or an indoor archery contest for kids to introduce them to those sports. That will make a great story opportunity with good visuals. Do your research to show reporters how archery is rising in popularity and how many kids go geocaching each year. You've just turned the same old expo into an opportunity for a trend story.

Does your church publish a cookbook? Well, so does every other house of worship in your town. There's nothing newsworthy about that. But what if you hold a cooking contest based around your cookbook's theme or solicit local restaurant chefs for demos at the farmers' market?

One of my favorite events when I worked as a reporter was the annual state fair. It lasted 10 days, so we had to come up with a new angle every day. Lots of my colleagues wanted to do the easy stories on the rides or the fried-things-on-a-stick or the largest-watermelon contest. The political reporter always did the story about politicians campaigning at the fair.

One year, I asked a simple question: What happens to all the manure from the hundreds of animals competing there? That question led to a fun front-page story introducing readers to the constant poop-disposal efforts and showing them what it's like to be a teenage exhibitor. Another year, I planned out my story in advance and did pre-fair interviews with the judges of the animal competitions who traveled from across the country to help young people hone their passion for working with livestock. Think like a reporter to find those unexpected, offbeat stories.

Behind the Scenes

If you have good relationships with some solid reporters, try inviting them behind the scenes of your event. Journalists love seeing the curtain being pulled back from something everyone takes for granted, and their readers and viewers love the chance to learn something they didn't know.

Two of my former newspaper colleagues had a lot of fun for several years with a regular feature called "Anything Once"—the idea being that they'd try something once, spending a day in the shoes of a particular profession and then writing and producing videos about it. They got to conduct a wedding, decorate cupcakes, and work alongside a locksmith. I substituted once and got to work as an apple-picker on a local farm—it's much harder than it looks.

One of my favorite stories that I've ever read was a feature by a local newspaper reporter in Ohio, near the Great Lakes, who rode along on a Coast Guard icebreaking vessel and wrote about what the men and women there did every day to keep shipping channels open. It was powerfully written and took readers onto the decks of the ship as it tore through the ice—but that glimpse into the lives and work of the Coast Guard would not have happened if the service hadn't been willing to open its doors and have him on board.

There are certainly risks to this approach. You have to trust the reporter and news outlet you're working with. You also need to agree to terms up front, especially if you work in sensitive areas. Educators deal with a lot of confidential information, as do many client-focused nonprofits. But there are ways of navigating confidentiality and privacy with proper legal guidance. Don't let that stand in the way of telling your great story.

From an image perspective, you need to make sure that what's visible behind the scenes supports the story and messages you're try-ing to get out—and at the very least, doesn't distract from that. This doesn't mean that you need to sanitize your workplace or restrict who the reporter talks to. But you do need to ensure that the people they speak with are prepared and comfortable with their roles as spokes-people for your organization. Your volunteer coordinator should be clear on what he can and cannot say about the challenges of recruiting new after-school program aides, for example. Your summer day-camp director must understand what topics she should avoid and which ones she should emphasize. You also need to make certain that any photos or video taken reflect the best side of your programs. A simple tidying-up can do wonders for a busy warehouse space or staff break room.

Preparing with Points

We introduced you to talking points in Chapter 7 in the context of interviews. Here's what you need to know about talking points specifically at an event.

The best speakers don't memorize their remarks. They speak from a combination of experience, knowledge of the subject, and their ability to read the room and play to the audience.

Note that we used the word "remarks" rather than "speeches." At most events, no one is giving a speech, as we usually think about it. That sort of speech inevitably brings with it a high degree of formality, not to mention pretentiousness. (The exceptions might be at a political event or convention, or any event where the president is speaking.)

Remarks at a typical local media event are usually less formal: You talk about the importance of the issue, tell a story, recall the history, create a personal connection, use a little humor if appropriate, and thank all the partners for their drive and effort. In the process, you give reporters attending the event some great quotes, background, and context for their stories.

Public speaking is terrifying for many people. It doesn't have to be. Many great organizations, such as Toastmasters, can help remove that fear and give you confidence.

For people who may have even minor concerns about saying the right things in the right manner, talking points are your friend. Rather than a full scripted speech, talking points are bulleted items that help you remember the essence of your remarks. They're highlights to help you organize your thoughts and stay on track. Include items such as elected officials you need to thank and VIPs you need to introduce.

Once you're up behind the lectern, talking points transform into a quick reference guide if you lose your train of thought or want to make sure you cite that statistic correctly. Have them in a simple folder, loose and not stapled, so you can flip the page quickly. Print them in a large, clean font and double-space them so you don't have to squint or bend your head down.

If you're writing talking points for someone else, ask about their preferences. Some speakers want complete sentences, while others like key words and phrases to jog their memory.

If you're organizing an event with multiple speakers, get copies of their talking points in advance and keep them at the lectern just in case someone forgets to bring them. In my years of doing PR, I've had someone use my complete talking points only once—when a high-profile elected official arrived at an event without the talking points I'd sent to his office a few days before. Luckily, I had an extra copy ready for them. They read my words verbatim—but that rarely happens.

Talking points can also include critical event details, such as where local residents will be standing (to the speaker's left or right?) and which button turns on the microphone (and accounting for people with color blindness who can't tell green from red). Even if you've practiced, don't count on your speaker remembering all those details when they get up in front of a crowd.

Don't Count on Speeches

Years ago, the media could be counted on to cover speeches given by elected officials, addresses from business leaders, and keynote remarks by others at conventions, meetings, and conferences. The speech itself, and the identity of the speaker, were the only draw needed.

That doesn't happen anymore. A speech has to be a big deal with actual news value. If you have a national-name expert or celebrity at your event, you might get the local media to attend. Most local papers don't even cover a CEO's remarks at the Chamber of Commerce any longer.

You may have a manager or C-suite executive who thinks that it's still the 1950s, and the media should be hanging on their every word. You'll need to break it to them gently that's no longer the case.

There are two exceptions: First, if you have a true national-name speaker coming to your local or regional event. If you can pull a Hollywood celebrity or a national leader, and if they're delivering a message of importance, then you might have a shot. Double those chances if you can get the local press to have a few minutes for a one-on-one interview with the speaker after they get off the stage. And second, if you can livestream the event so reporters don't have to physically attend. Sitting in a ballroom waiting for lunch to be served is dead time to a reporter.

Secrets of a Good Bill-Signing

If your organization has any interaction with state or local governments, you may be called upon at some point to host or be involved in an official signing ceremony of a bill or ordinance. Governors and mayors love the pomp and circumstance of signing legislation outside a stuffy office—and the attention from the media that comes with a good story. The same applies to proclamations, recognitions, and celebrations—any official document that can be signed. They're a good way to get positive news out. Even though the media will likely have covered the legislation while it went through committees, hearings, and votes, the signing puts the final feather in the cap and brings it to a close.

Your role may vary with this type of event. You might be hosting the entire thing from soup to nuts; you could be providing speakers and real people to talk about the impact the new law will make; or you may just be providing a friendly location with a great backdrop. Your governor's or mayor's staff will have most of the details worked out and be able to work with you on their needs.

A few necessities for your bill-signing checklist:

TABLE AND CHAIRS At most signing ceremonies, the signer— let's call them the governor for simplicity's sake—will be seated at a long table with the official text in front of them. A standard folding table will usually work fine. Get a nice stable non-wheeled chair for them to sit in; avoid institutional-looking folding metal chairs if at all possible. If you have older people, small children, or people with physical disabilities in the core group, have another chair or two on hand in case it's needed.

TABLE COVERING The governor's office may have a fabric covering that it uses to drape over the table and cover up table legs, the governor's legs, and anything else. This often has a logo or slogan on it to draw the eye. Depending on the circumstances, your organization may be asked to provide the table covering with your logo or name. Make sure it's freshly laundered, gets hung up for storage, and doesn't have telltale fold lines. If you need one, simple primary colors that match your organization's branding are the best; they can be purchased for $100–$300, depending on quality, size, and details of your logo.

PENS The governor's office will often supply the pens, but have a few extras on hand just in case of emergencies. Some signing ceremonies will involve a different pen being used for each letter of the person's name, which allows the signer to give an official pen to multiple VIPs, speakers, or people who were especially instrumental in passing the bill.

OTHER TABLE DÉCOR Generally you'll want the signing table to be as simple as possible, but occasionally an item is needed— such as something that illustrates the problem the bill will be solving. Check with the governor's staff on what they want.

ROOM FOR STANDING The governor typically signs the bill surrounded by a delegation of other elected officials—the bill's sponsors—as well as some real people that it will affect, organizations that played a role, or members of the Cabinet who will be carrying out the law. Make sure your area has room for those people to stand and get in the official photographs. Don't place the signing table back against a wall with no space for the supporters.

BACKGROUND IMAGES As at any media event, check and double-check your background. An antipollution bill signed at the edge of a lake is great—but not when a motorboat starts zipping by at top speed. If a small-business bill is being signed inside a small business, take down the "50% Off Sale" sign so it doesn't appear to be hanging over the governor's head.

LECTERN You should check to see if speakers will be talking from behind a lectern (often incorrectly called a podium). The governor's staff will probably provide one if needed, but your organization may want to purchase one to have on hand for future events. They're available for $100–$300, depending on size and level of fanciness.

AUDIO AMPLIFICATION Elected officials are old hats at being heard above a crowd—speaking is what they do for a living. But if you have representatives of your business or nonprofit speaking, or students from your school, get a portable PA system set up and working in advance so they can be heard clearly.

Virtual Events

During the pandemic, everyone who was used to staging elaborate shindigs in person had to immediately pivot to virtual events—media events, to be sure, but also full conferences, workshops, seminars, classes, and more. Many are planning to keep using such events moving forward.

The best thing about a virtual event is that it allows you to potentially attract far more people—both attendees and speakers. You can get authors, experts, and politicians from all across the country without the cost of transportation and putting them up at a hotel, and they can fit multiple speaking engagements into a day from the comfort of their home office.

The worst thing is that a poorly organized event can come across like the most boring Zoom meeting in history, and you don't want that. Yours should be memorable for the right reasons.

The special art of holding a virtual event requires perhaps even more planning, practice, and precision than an in-person one. Here are some key factors to keep in mind:

BACKGROUNDS AND LIGHTING Virtual backgrounds can be good, providing a unifying theme for all the speakers, or bad, creating strange visuals around the edges of a speaker's head and body. Lighting can be great and natural or awful, making your speaker look like a vampire. Check everyone's setting out in advance and don't be afraid to give friendly suggestions to problematic participants.

TEST CALLS If possible, do a test call under the conditions you're going to be holding the event. Participants and speakers should dial in from the computers they're going to be using, in the rooms where they're going to be using them. A regular news conference or bill-signing may not need a run-through, but a major event with your state's US senator may. The staff of the VIPs can log in to do the test so you're not taking up their bosses' time.

CHAT If you're taking questions from the audience or the media, a chat function is the best way to handle submissions. You avoid crosstalk and the awkwardness of "You go first," "No, you," etc. It also lets you do a little screening of problematic questions and enables you to keep the microphone away from that particular kind of person who wants to lecture rather than ask a real question.

TECH GREMLINS Without a doubt, you'll have some technical glitches of unknown origin to deal with—the speaker's audio going dead, a presenter's slide deck not in synch with their words, or just a videoconference platform that can't handle the number of people trying to join. That's why dry run-throughs and test calls are so important. For high-profile events, have your IT staff standing close by for last-minute assistance.

MUTE ALL There's always someone in a group who doesn't understand the concept of muting their line; before video chats, it was conference calls. When you have multiple speakers, use the mute-all function to keep things quiet and toggle the individual speakers on and off manually. That's the best way to keep things on track.

DESIGNATE AN ADMIN If you're speaking, managing the content, or tracking time, it's best practice to handle the administrative and hosting sides of the event to another trusted person. You can be there in the same room side-by-side, but someone else should have their eyes and hands on the wheel.

The Celebrity Factor

On some occasions, you may have the opportunity to hold an event with a real celebrity in attendance—a sports star whose off-the-court advocacy mirrors your nonprofit's work, or a Hollywood actor who has an endorsement deal with your business franchise, for example. Celebrities can add value to an event, drawing both the public and the media.

You need to make sure that their star power doesn't overwhelm your core message, however. If the media sends its NBA reporter to cover the event just to talk with the basketball player, chances are good your work and the broader issues they're there to draw attention to are likely to be ignored. Work with the celebrity's staff in advance to make sure they have your talking points and are willing to reposition the conversation back to focus on you. It's also bad form to have the celebrity's attendance be the sole purpose for your event. Develop some other news angle to pitch so that there's at least the aura of a greater goal at hand.

Sometimes, you may get a celebrity in attendance who doesn't want a media circus there. That should be respected, but there are ways to showcase their support for your organization after the fact. When I worked for a local school system, one year the high school graduation speaker was country music star Jimmie Allen, who had a family member in the graduating class. Owing to pandemic restrictions, we weren't able to have the media there, but I took a whole fleet of photos, wrote a comprehensive story, and sent them out to our local outlets, which in turn showcased both Allen and the school's new graduates.

THE TAKEAWAY

Running a media event is almost never like it looks in the movies. Remember that the main goal is to help tell your story—everything else flows from that.

- Think creatively, from your choice of speakers to your visuals. Don't do things the way they've always been done.
- Coordinate your speakers and check their talking points so there's no overlap.
- Use a checklist for your logistics so the event runs smoothly.
- For virtual events, have an extra pair of hands controlling the technical side so you can focus on the content and schedule.

Perhaps most importantly: Have an inclement weather plan. A sunny day can turn into thunderstorms faster than you can wrap things up and sprint for the parking lot.

"I'll only do things that fit our mission"

Karen Foster is executive director of All Out Adventures, a local non-profit in Massachusetts that helps people of all ages and abilities experience the outdoors. In a normal year, Foster's small team runs about 180 programs serving 750 people across the Commonwealth.

After time as a high school teacher, Foster leveraged her love of the outdoors and backpacking into certifications and training that would allow her to teach skiing, handle first-aid emergencies, and more. She started with All Out Adventures as an instructor, then worked as development manager, and then moved into the executive director's role. "I've really had to learn all the parts of running a nonprofit," she says, including administration, fundraising, and finances—and public relations.

Working in the outdoors, Foster's organization has a great natural backdrop to work with for events that attract the media. She's selective with events, careful not to take on too much. "The thing that's so incredibly important to me is that I'll really only do things that fit our mission. It's always going to be accessible to the people who use our programs," she says. All Out Adventures has two main events that have gotten a good degree of attention from the press, but neither of them started out that way.

The longest-running event, the Kayak-a-Thon, is just what it sounds like—a waterborne trip that raises money for the organization. "It's what we do [regularly], just for a whole lot more people and a longer distance," Foster says. It took about seven or eight years of running the event before she was able to get the media to attend, largely because the paddlers' arrival time was so approximate. "I could say we were going to land at 3 p.m., but it might not be until 4 p.m.," she says. Then one year, a single outlet decided it would be worth it. "They started coming, and it became this self-fulfilling thing. They came and saw how cool it was, and then came back the next year, and then other news media started picking it up and it sort of grew from there."

The other event, the Plunge, involves community leaders and All Out staff jumping into frigid water—after chainsawing through inches of ice—to raise both donations and awareness. The first year was a test run; the second got community influencers involved, such as city council members, real estate agents, restaurant owners. This was one event where Foster had to work hard to get attention due to the remote location of the event. "We generated all that on our own," she says. "It was a news release and photos, and they got interested and ran a story ahead of time and again afterwards, and were pretty charmed by the whole thing."

Other reporters have covered their more routine events, including adaptive bike rides, snowshoeing treks, and more. "I always make myself available at events. If they're coming, I make sure I'm there too," Foster advises. "I make it really easy for them—hosting them, making sure I had the correct spelling of names. . . . If they call me, I call them back immediately, give them my personal phone number."

What's the impact of media events on the organization's bottom line? Foster discusses another recent event that attracted a good deal of media coverage, a daylong kayak event along the Connecticut River with local elected officials and other VIPs. "It was really kind of a power-player event, and it got full-page media coverage," Foster recalled. "For three or so weeks after that, I would get people saying, 'I saw you in the paper,' or a website inquiry. What it does is keep you more in the consciousness. We'll get a donation I wasn't expecting, a few hundred dollars here and there, but it's more that it keeps people in the community feeling like they know us and like us and support us. I don't ever look at a media thing and say, 'This didn't translate to dollars.' I play the big picture, long game with that."

— 9 —

CURVEBALLS AND CRISES

Smithville

Lydia Norwood is executive director of the Smithville Heritage Association, a nonprofit that runs a museum and organizes educational programs showcasing the community's Native American history. Her staff of 10 handles everything from curriculum development and accounting to grant-writing and museum tours. One day in June, in the middle of a planning meeting for the upcoming Heritage Festival, she's interrupted by an urgent call from her panicked IT manager. The group's cloud service provider has been hacked and its donor lists, program rosters, and payment information of vendors and visitors have all been exposed online, with bank information, addresses, and phone numbers all breached. It's part of a national hack, and about 5 million people across the country are affected.

In any organization, you will have challenges, and inevitably some of them will be crises.

State budget cuts will hurt your food bank's clients. An employee will embezzle money from your antique shop. One of your teachers will be accused of sexual misconduct.

Crises happen every day; how you recover from them depends in large part on how you communicate about them—and how transparent you are. This chapter gives hands-on advice and practical information on steering the ship through a crisis and talking about it in a way that builds confidence in your ability to recover. Preparing an institution to weather a crisis requires a hands-on tactical focus, a broad strategic view, media savvy, and the ability to research, absorb, and turn out information quickly and efficiently.

How you communicate details during a crisis is almost as important as how your organization responds and reacts overall. It doesn't matter if the actions your business takes are picture-perfect if no one knows about them. If your school takes immediate action to get rid of a staffer who committed some misconduct but doesn't share that with anyone, it's like it never happened—and can look like a cover-up even if that wasn't the intention. Always remember that reporters don't *have* to wait for you to tell a story—if you're not communicating information, they'll get it from another source.

Handling communications and marketing at a Delaware electric utility, Jeremy Tucker has had to deal with his share of power outages. One year, the utility's system malfunctioned and residents of several neighborhoods had to deal with damage to expensive home electronics, including computers and various appliances.

The utility company was up front with its customers, Tucker says. "We immediately acknowledged our errors, explained to those impacted the steps we were taking to address the problems, and offered financial assistance to customers with damaged equipment. We were proactive, apologetic, and honest."

What Is a Crisis?

It's easy to recognize a crisis when you're in the middle of it. It's not so simple to identify one in advance. A crisis, at its core, is a situation or event that threatens the existence or future of your organization. A small crisis for one organization may be a huge crisis for another; the dynamics all depend on your specific organization and its structure, role, and needs.

Most crisis-communication case studies focus on national brands or major natural disasters. Those examples don't always provide the guidance you need for handling local issues. Here are a few examples of crises that could occur on the local level along with potential threats that could arise from them:

Two elected officials get into a fistfight at the political party headquarters.

WHAT'S AT STAKE: The party's reputation and the officials' authority as leaders.

A respected nonprofit organization is accused of falsifying records for a government contract in a lawsuit filed by a whistleblower.

WHAT'S AT STAKE: Financial stability and the organization's reputation in the area.

A property developer with several high-profile projects in the pipeline is accused of sexual harassment by employees.

WHAT'S AT STAKE: Willingness of other companies to partner with the developer and complete current projects, leading to financial risks.

A mobile app used by a school district is reported to have security flaws that exposed staff's personal information, including Social Security numbers.

WHAT'S AT STAKE: Immediate risk to staff's identities and finances, as well as damage to the district's reputation.

The industry or sector you work in will determine your most likely potential crises. Here are general examples of some common or universal the types of crises you may find yourself involved in and should prepare for:

- chemical leaks
- building collapse
- workplace violence
- active shooter
- bomb threat
- flooding
- fire
- food-borne illness
- product safety issue
- hacking or IT security breach
- political protests
- lawsuits
- embezzlement or financial misdeeds

Sometimes you'll find yourself dealing with a crisis that doesn't directly threaten your organization. You may be in a role as a regulator, providing oversight, or a supplier to a company involved in a crisis. The same principles in this chapter apply to those situations as well.

Crisis-Planning Principles

Regardless of the type of crisis, you should center your plan around some key principles:

> **TIMELINESS** Communication in a crisis must be prompt and efficient. If your news releases are slow to reach the press, you're going to lose. Have as much content pre-written as possible to help you act as quickly as you can.

> **ACCURACY** When you create your draft releases, FAQs, and talking points, they should be in as final a form as possible, including review by your organization's subject-matter experts

and leadership. You don't want to be in the position of checking basic facts while in the middle of a PR storm.

UNIFIED MESSAGING This principle is especially important when you're working with partners or others that share common interests, such as a trade association or allied government agency. In such a dynamic, everyone needs to be working from the same playbook. The media should have a single point of contact to eliminate confusion. All stakeholders must receive the same messages. Unified hashtags and use of a single website for showcasing updates and information can help with coordinating the public-facing messaging.

Make It a Team Effort

Even if you're the only person directly handling communications in a crisis, you're not alone. Your organization should have both a crisis management team and a crisis communication team to help you navigate the process properly. Tap the expertise of your executive leadership and legal counsel. If you have a marketing staffer who handles things like branding, advertising, and outreach, include them as well. Put this team together well ahead of a crisis and run through responses to different scenarios. Make sure everyone understands their role in a crisis and what latitude they have to do their jobs.

People outside your organization can be part of your team too, in a way. Make certain that you have excellent relationships with your first responders, including law enforcement, firefighters, and medical personnel. If you have a crisis that touches on their areas, expect that they may be sharing the initial information with the media. Ask questions about their processes and what they disclose. Get their contact information and keep it on hand.

Off-site Locations

If you have an on-site crisis—something that must be handled then and there—then you don't want to bring the media there for a briefing.

Consider an active shooter situation at a school; for purely safety reasons, you want reporters as far away as possible. Reporters will show up at your main offices or location to get whatever information they can.

Identify several predetermined nearby backup locations to bring the media to. When I worked with a school district, I had several options—including a county government building, a community college conference center, and the local fire hall—that would be good locations for media staging. These briefing sites will pull the media away from the action, protecting the privacy of families, victims, and others. When I covered the murder of a local police officer, the mayor and other officials held a briefing at the county government's emergency operations center, miles away from where the search for a wanted person was taking place. That ensured everyone's safety and kept us reporters out of the searchers' hair.

Long-Term Issues Management

In public relations, the rather vague term "issues management" refers to the art of anticipating and preparing for longer-term, big-picture strategic threats and trends. An issue is something that you can reasonably see coming down the road. The threat may be one or two years away, but you need to start preparing for it now, before it becomes a major crisis. In some cases, if you're lucky, the work you do to prepare may mitigate the actual crisis. Issues management involves significant long-term investments of time and energy, which you may never see returned; this can be a hard sell to executives or leaders.

When I came on board as communications director at the Delaware Department of Agriculture, one of the primary issues that the entire team was preparing for was a possible outbreak of bird flu, or avian influenza. Because the state has more than 700 poultry farmers who create thousands of jobs and billions of dollars of economic impact, that was a big deal. If there was an outbreak, it would be important to project confidence, authority, and leadership in the face of a deadly disease. Given the spread of the disease around the globe, it was not a question of *if* it would come to tiny Delaware but *when*. This was the perfect situation for which to start an issues management process.

We had very little in the way of communications tools and plans— one PowerPoint presentation and a basic news release template. I started working on this from the ground up, immersing myself in avian influenza information. I met with our animal-health staff and talked about it for hours. I sat in on planning meetings. I read materials from other states and the federal government. I read a book about bird flu by a critic of animal farmers, to see how opponents might view the situation.

To create the plan, I used the publicly available framework created by the US Department of Agriculture and matched our five key messages to theirs. I brainstormed everything I would need if I were stationed for a week on-site at a remote rural farm where avian influenza had been discovered. Then I wrote out the plan under the assumption I had won the lottery and quit the next day, and the person having to do the work had zero background knowledge. I wrote talking points, draft news releases, social media posts, fact sheets, timelines, checklists, and more.

Once the plan was created and approved, and after I'd practically memorized the whole thing, we went on the road, doing outreach to university staff, agricultural businesses, educators, and staff at our environmental and health agencies—anyone who would be in a position to pick up the phone during an outbreak and have a reporter ask them questions.

I invited my counterparts to a meeting representing all the agencies involved in the actual response planning, including the state universities, the National Guard, our transportation agency, county governments, and the communications teams for the major chicken companies. We took an entire morning and I walked them through our response plan and major communications points. We also set up an email list so that in an outbreak, anything I sent out for public consumption would also go to them—going back to the unified messaging principles we discussed earlier.

After I started sitting in on agency planning meetings and learning more about the effect of this horrific disease and what it did to our animals, I had a few sleepless nights worrying about how I would respond, imagining myself in front of reporters with my mouth hanging open and nothing to say—or worse, saying the wrong thing and affecting the livelihoods of thousands of Delaware families. After the communications plan was put in place, I slept like a baby. It was all about knowing that we were ready and having something to rely on.

Coordination in Planning

You will often encounter crises that have overlapping effects or jurisdictions. These require a high degree of coordination and planning. For example, one year when I was working with our state's agriculture agency, a crop-duster pilot accidentally sprayed some pesticides on a crew of road workers patching potholes on a country road. We had four government agencies involved: mine, because we regulated pesticides and handled spray complaints; our environmental agency, because of the possible effect on the environment and their decontamination operations; the health department, because of the human health factor; and the transportation agency, which employed the workers who were sprayed. On the local level, there were also fire companies and ambulance crews involved as first responders.

Under other circumstances, it might have taken a long time to sort out who had jurisdiction. But because the communications staff from all the agencies knew each other, we pulled together a rapid conference call and established that my agency's pesticide team would be the lead investigator. We quickly mapped out the basic facts and created a communications strategy. Each agency would release the facts from its work on the scene—which were coordinated so one agency didn't accidentally contradict the other. When one of us replied to a reporter, we copied the other communications staff so everyone knew what was being said at all times. Since my agency was investigating the overall incident, I was designated as the media point of contact moving forward. Thankfully, the effects were minimal and the workers were all fine.

This is an example of how important planning is. Even simple networking with contacts from other organizations, businesses, and government agencies can help streamline your crisis response. Since we all knew and had met each other, we all understood each other's roles. If we were still exchanging cell numbers and emails on day one of the accident, we would have found ourselves in a much more difficult situation.

What's in Your Plan?

When you are developing your crisis communications plans, the end result should be both practical and focused on meeting the organization's specific needs. Ignore the online templates that insist on bland, generic statements and foundational elements. You need a living, breathing document that contains the protocols, procedures, items, and resources you'll need in an emergency. You won't be able to create materials that cover every eventuality in a crisis, but you will be able to build content that puts you on a solid footing from the start and buys you time to write and craft material that *is* situation-specific.

Here are the elements I include in every crisis communications plan that I develop:

- [ ] **social media:** Posts, images, graphics, and videos
- [ ] **web content:** Text, images, and videos that you can instantly drop onto a page to create a one-stop information source for the public
- [ ] **alerts:** Text messages and e-blasts
- [ ] **fact sheets** and backgrounders

- [ ] **letters** from organizational leadership to key stakeholders or the public
- [ ] **public service announcement scripts** and recorded audio and video spots
- [ ] **news release drafts**
- [ ] **talking points**
- [ ] **updated media contact lists**
- [ ] **event logistics** plans and checklists
- [ ] **location maps**
- [ ] **photographs**

Once your planning is well under way, take a moment to think about other content you might need. You may want to put more time into creating educational or explainer articles that help the public understand the challenge and what they can do. You may want to pre-record your leadership delivering messages of concern or sympathy so you don't have to pull them out of the conference room mid-crisis.

Smithville

IN ACTION: Lydia walks into her office and pulls her crisis communications plan off the shelf. There's no section specifically about a national hack of confidential information, but it does have language that includes reassuring statements to clients and customers. While her IT manager assesses the damage and makes sure their information is now safe, Lydia works with her communications manager to create an email notifying their donors and members whose information was exposed about the problem and assuring that the association is doing everything it can to keep their information safe. For the media, they create a news release—known as a holding statement—sharing that same information, just in a different format and with different language. This will be the first that her local media hears about any Smithville-specific impacts, so they need to make sure the release has the right context, frames the problem appropriately, and isn't likely to trigger mass concern.

Get Outside Assistance

In a crisis, you'll often have a feeling of being alone—as though you're the only person or group of people dealing with the situation. Thankfully, that's not the case. There's always an option to get outside aid and counsel. Sometimes all you need is an extra brain to bounce ideas off; at other times, you need high-level expert advice on specific situations. In still other circumstances, you need bodies to staff the phones and triage media calls. There are a few main avenues for obtaining help:

COMPETITORS You may be scratching your head right now. Competitors helping you out? Yes. In a situation that could touch the entire industry, your competitor firms and nonprofits in your field may be your best source of outside advice. They know your business and sector-specific details. They have a vested interest in ensuring that the crisis doesn't spread. They may not be able to lend you people or resources, but they can certainly be a sounding board for planning and coordination.

TRADE AND INDUSTRY ASSOCIATIONS Chances are good that your industry's trade associations have heard of this kind of crisis before and can offer guidance or suggestions. Check with staff and leadership on the state and national levels immediately. They may have a pre-built crisis communication toolkit that you can tap into. In some cases, the association may already have a communications firm on retainer to help its members. When I worked for a school district, our state school board association had a Pennsylvania company standing by that specialized in school public relations and marketing and offered free assistance to member school districts on crisis communications. You're paying for that through your dues and membership fees, so use it.

STATE AND LOCAL EMERGENCY MANAGEMENT AGENCIES Each state and county, and sometimes larger cities, will have a public agency set up to handle emergencies and disasters. These agencies are typically coordinators—they don't have hundreds or thousands of workers who handle the physical work of recovery and rebuilding from hurricanes or floods. Rather, their expertise is in planning and managing resources contributed from other public agencies and private businesses, such as members of the National Guard, nonprofit volunteers, or doctors and nurses who handle public health issues. Depending on the situation, you may be able to ask your local emergency agency for assistance, or at least guidance and advice. They will typically have at least one person dedicated to public information who can likely give you some good counsel. At the very least, these agencies offer training that can be free or at a minimal cost to private-sector businesses or nonprofits. (See below for more details.)

CRISIS COMMUNICATIONS FIRMS In the realm of public-relations consultants, there is a specialized subset of companies that only handle crisis management and communications. These firms can be expensive, and there's no guarantee of results in this field, but they do have real-world experience in managing through a crisis and making it go away that you might find valuable. If you're in need of professional counsel, ask your local Public Relations Society of America (PRSA) chapter for a referral to find out who in your area has the best reputation and results.

Train, Train, Train

There's an often-cited and widely attributed quote in the military about training: "The more you sweat in training, the less you bleed in combat." Take that to heart in your crisis communications planning. Every agency or business is going to have a crisis at some point. That is a guarantee. The only question is how prepared you will be.

While there are training programs available for you and your team, training for a crisis doesn't end with going to a one-day seminar. Preparation must become part of your regular routine. If you don't keep your skills and information fresh, you're going to forget critical details or overlook connections when you're in the heat of an emergency. Establish a regular time each week to review your plans, read an article, write new talking points, record a video, take online training, or brainstorm possible problems and solutions with other people in your organization. If you don't keep things current, then you'll pull out your crisis plan two years down the road and realize 75 percent of that once-great plan is now outdated and useless.

Those local and state emergency management agencies we mentioned earlier often have formal training opportunities to teach business and nonprofit representatives the basics of communicating in an emergency. When I worked in state government, I sat in workshops alongside people from fire companies, casinos, airports, and electric utilities. We didn't have much in common on the outside, but we shared the desire to learn more about how to prepare our organizations—and ourselves—for the disasters we knew were lurking just around the corner.

I recommend starting with the basic, free online independent-study courses offered through the Federal Emergency Management Agency (training.fema.gov/is/). The foundational courses, which help you understand the structure of local emergency management, are Introduction to the Incident Command System and Introduction to the National Incident Management System. These are fairly dense courses and very heavy in bureaucratic terminology, but it's language you need to understand if you'll be working in future crises. It'll help you understand what your local law enforcement, fire companies, hospitals, and other agencies are talking about. Also available online at this writing are an awareness course for public information officers and a course on using social media in emergencies.

The Rural Domestic Preparedness Consortium (ruraltraining.org) offers a "Working with the Media" course online; it's intended for first responders in rural areas, but it has lessons applicable to anyone in any industry or sector.

Moving to the in-person realm, check with your local or state emergency management agency on the availability of courses like basic public information officer training. You'll walk away with binders full of advice and information and sometimes with pocket-size reference material that can be stuffed into a backpack in a pinch.

In-person courses are valuable in no small part due to the professional networking that occurs as part of the training, creating invaluable connections for the future. Specialized emergency management and preparedness courses are also available for schools, agribusiness, farmers, sports facilities, and other sectors. This latter type of training doesn't just focus on communications but covers a wide range of topics that are extremely helpful. The in-person communications training is often oriented toward emergency management professionals and people who support them—people who work in law enforcement, the fire services, emergency medicine, government IT, utility companies, and the like. You may have to stretch or rewrite some of the materials to make them fit your specific needs—but that's fairly easy to do.

If you can't make a training session, search online for the course title and the phrase "student manual." You can often find the entire course handbook for free as a PDF, which is better than nothing in a disaster.

Train on Your Own

If you can't get into those training sessions, or don't find them helpful, you can still train on your own, using homemade resources. That was how I prepped for tough media interviews when I was readying for a bird flu outbreak, as we discussed earlier. To help get ready, I assembled my team and asked them to come up with tough questions about avian influenza, aka bird flu. Their backgrounds were in marketing, sales, and grant management, so they approached the issue much as a reporter would—with a little bit of information and a lot of assumptions that may or may not be correct.

Once they were ready, I sat on one side of a conference table. They sat on the other and peppered me with questions they would want to have answered if an outbreak were to hit Delaware. The questions were tough and real—asking about the impact on jobs, whether humans could catch the disease, and what exactly happened to the chickens. I answered them the best I could based on the weeks of full-time work I'd done to prepare and took notes on the areas where my answers were weak or insufficient. At the end, I had pages of items to research or add to. The exercise took only about an hour, but it was supremely valuable in helping prepare for all sorts of questions that were sure to come flying fast and furious once reporters got hold of the story. On a personal level, it also helped me prepare myself mentally for the prospect of being the recipient of a barrage of questions.

This type of training is simple and easy for anyone to do. Just gather a group of coworkers, family members, or friends who don't have deep background knowledge of the subject, and ask them to hit you with the hardest, strangest, and most out-of-the-blue questions they can summon up. Trust me, it'll help.

Continuity of Operations Planning

Your organization or business should have some sort of plan for maintaining your operations even if your city is flooded, your power is cut, your offices are unusable, or your executive director is suddenly struck down sick. This subset of crisis preparation is called continuity of operations planning, abbreviated as COOP. Entire books could be, and are, written about maintaining continuity in a disaster—but the point here is that your COOP should be integrated into your crisis communications plan. Many of the common crisis scenarios that you'll be planning for on the communications side—disruptions in supplies, lack of building access, etc.—also will be impacted by your leadership's operational decisions.

Ready, Set, Go

Some crises come at you like a fastball speeding at your head—no warning at all. For others, you may have advance warning of some form. Sometimes you can detect the shape of something that will evolve into a crisis later on—hopefully you'll spot it just early enough to do a little preparation.

You should use every second of the time you have to get ready:

1. Establish the facts.
2. Anticipate the scope and scale of the problem.
3. Determine what others know and will say about it.
4. Figure out a timeline.
5. Create your initial messaging and holding statements.

Holding Statements

A holding statement is the very first item you'll issue in a crisis. It's designed to calm the media beast, reassure your stakeholders and the public, and express empathy for anyone who was affected. It also has the added benefit of buying your organization a little more time to put out something more substantive. A holding statement should never be hanging out there by itself for an extended period of time.

Here's an example of a holding statement used by Lydia Norwood and her Smithville nonprofit group about the data breach:

> *We learned today that a security breach at Nile.com, which the Smithville Heritage Association uses for offsite data storage, exposed the personal information of about 500 donors, museum guests, program participants, and event sponsors. We are told this information may include names, addresses, phone numbers, and payment information.*

We deeply regret that our Smithville community members were affected by this hack, which also affected about 5 million other Americans. Protecting the confidentiality of our support-ers' and visitors' information is one of our highest priorities. We are taking immediate action to ensure that the remaining data is secure and to move it to a new vendor.

By Friday, our staff will reach out to all community mem-bers whose data was exposed. They may also be receiving a notification from Nile.com, which has agreed to pay for credit monitoring for anyone who wishes it.

We will be sharing more information as we receive it, includ-ing about how to sign up for credit monitoring with Nile.com.

We encourage members of the community to contact security@smithvilleheritage.org if they have any questions. All messages will receive a reply within 24 hours.

That statement includes an acknowledgment of the problem, an expression of empathy, details on what's being done to fix the prob-lem—even though they're sparse at that point—and promises to be in contact and respond quickly to questions. Follow-up messages might focus on the credit monitoring, the response from community mem-bers (if positive), and any more information learned about the breach.

Get in Front of the Story

Depending on the exact circumstance and dynamics, you may want to take control of the narrative and the timeline by getting out ahead of the story. That means breaking bad news yourself rather than leaving it up to the media. That will allow you to establish the initial narrative and frame the problem in your own terms, rather than having some-one else do it for you.

Sometimes self-disclosure can inoculate you sufficiently from the problem to make it all die down quietly. You'll have the high ground of transparency for a time. But more than likely, it won't be enough, just serving as the first salvo.

Give Regular Updates

When you're the primary source of information on a crisis or emergency, you'll be bombarded with inquiries and requests for updates from reporters at all hours of the day and night. Each media outlet has its own deadlines, and with the increasing emphasis on 24/7 online coverage, that deadline is almost always *right the heck now.*

To help manage the media and save your sanity, establish strict timetables for providing regular news. For example, tell the press you'll be providing a written update every morning at 10 a.m. and a livestreamed briefing at 3 p.m.—or whatever meshes with your operational needs and leadership direction. That won't completely stop the inquiries flooding your inbox and filling up your voice mail, but it will help dramatically if they can count on getting the basic information at a regular time every day. Just make sure that you're consistent and actually able to deliver the updates on that timetable. There are few things worse to deal with than reporters who have been promised information and then effectively ghosted.

As time goes by and reporters' interest flags, you can reduce the frequency to once daily, then twice weekly, then once weekly, and then trail them off entirely.

Smithville

IN ACTION: *The local TV news and newspapers hopped on Lydia's news release right away, as she expected. Her communications manager scheduled interviews with interested reporters and created talking points for Lydia to review to get the main elements cemented in her mind. The first stories reported are restrained, simple, matter-of-fact reports about the problem. But with the Heritage Festival coming up, Lydia is concerned about donors' and sponsors' confidence in the organization. Even though the data breach occurred with one of their vendors, the nonprofit is still ultimately responsible for the confidentiality of the information.*

For her next step, Lydia confers with her IT manager to select a new vendor to handle their offsite data storage, and oversees the transfer of all their information to this new, trusted company. She makes personal calls to top donors and event sponsors to reassure them that the organization is taking quick action, and asks one prominent sponsor to help them reassure others. Before the next festival planning meeting, she invites the local reporters who covered the story at first for a sit-down interview with her, the nonprofit board chair, their IT manager, and the sponsor, to talk about how the community can be assured that their information is safe. The resulting articles and TV reports are positive and run at a critical time in the festival planning process. Her team reports that donors appreciated the personal outreach and the media coverage and that the festival's finances will not take a hit this year as a result.

You Don't Always Need to Respond

You'll encounter some situations that sure feel like crises. You'll have people stirred up in a tizzy and reporters calling and badgering you and your team. The temptation will be there to always treat all crises the same and pull out all the stops. I understand—it's baked into my DNA to want to talk to all reporters, all the time, and be as transparent as possible. But it's not always the best thing for you.

Before you start to make your calls, take a deep breath and look and listen:

- Is this actually a crisis?
- What is escalating passions?
- What does the media really want?
- Who's the main source of information on this now?

You may find that what feels like a real crisis is actually an artificial media-induced feeding frenzy. The relative impact on your organization may in reality be minimal. Take a deep breath and ask yourself: Do you really need to respond?

As a former journalist I hate to say this, but it's not always in your best interest to talk to the media. You do lose control of a little bit of *your* story every time a reporter writes *their* story. And in some cases, your organization can be tainted simply by association with another crisis.

So before you get wrapped up in a faux crisis brought on by an aggressive reporter or a producer with an axe to grind or airtime to fill, think carefully about whether you even need to talk to them.

Be Ready for the Aftermath

In my reporting days, I was once part of a team covering a truly horrific crime. I won't go into the details, but the victims were children and the criminal was a person who had been highly trusted in the community. This was a crime of evil.

A few days after the initial news had come out, I attended a news conference organized by the state prosecutor to provide the latest information on the investigation. We gathered in a cramped, dark conference room in a Department of Justice office building and got the standard briefing.

After it was over, I approached one of the prosecutors who specialized in crimes against children, standing off in a corner of the room. I noticed that they hadn't discussed the number of victims; at that point, we all thought it just involved one or two kids. How many children, I asked the prosecutor, do you suspect were victimized?

Around a hundred, she replied.

In that instant, the news transformed from an awful but relatively small story into a horrible crisis that would turn lives upside down and transform a community.

The attorneys and staff handling the case had what I'd later realize was a thousand-yard-stare; I'm not sure if the prosecutor realized the enormity of what she was saying in the moment, or even if she was authorized to say it. But it wasn't the type of information that could be hidden.

Having a plan to control the disclosure of important information until you can process the big picture gives you a greater understanding of what will follow after major news becomes public—and help you determine the effects and consequences in the aftermath. That can make a tremendous difference to your community.

Don't Panic

It's easy to identify a crisis when you're in the middle of handling communications. Phones are ringing, your email is dinging, social media is blowing up, and your boss is panicking. You have that little acid-reflux feeling in the middle of your chest and it's rising higher into your throat every minute. Your hands are clammy and your scalp is sweating. And you probably have to go to the bathroom pretty urgently.

Those situations and symptoms can be an indicator or a trigger of panic—and panicking is the last thing you want to do in a crisis. As the communications leader, you have to keep cool, calm, and collected. You don't want your team, your bosses, or especially the media to see that you're feeling nervous, anxious, eaten up inside, or absolutely terrified.

It is perfectly normal to feel all those things in a crisis! I would be surprised if you didn't. You just can't let anyone on the outside see that, or let those feelings influence your decision-making. Poor decisions can lead to even more negative outcomes down the road. "Fatigue, fear, and panic undermine our ability to think clearly and creatively, manage our relationships effectively, focus attention on the right priorities, and make smart, informed choices," write consultants and trainers Tony Schwartz and Emily Pines in the *Harvard Business Review*. That's not an environment in which you want to be making snap decisions that can affect the livelihoods of all your employees and many more constituents.

Schwartz and Pines outline a four-step approach to getting control and beating back panic:

1. Be actively aware of your feelings, recognizing and naming them.
2. Use breath or movement to calm your physical body down.
3. Talk to your "adult self" and help that part of you care for your "overwhelmed self." Acknowledge your feelings, but state simply that they are temporary.
4. Stick to the facts; don't let the story or narrative that you're experiencing take charge.

I've often found that taking a five-minute walk can help dramatically with staying calm in a crisis. You're not abandoning your post but rather taking the time you need to get back in control. In the long run, you'll be better ready to handle whatever needs handling.

Focus on Recovery

Your initial communications in a crisis—the holding statement and the first few releases of information—need to be about having control over the immediate situation. Once the threat has passed or is dissipating, however, the majority of your focus as a communicator needs to be on recovery. That creates a bridge between what has happened—the crisis that you may not be able to directly control—and what will happen—all the actions that you are taking moving forward.

Emergency managers speak of a "recovery continuum," covering the short term (days), the intermediate term (weeks or months), and the long term (months and years). Too often in communications we focus on what's directly in front of us—that's just how the job works—and lose sight of what's coming down the road. As early as possible, you should work on anticipating your communications needs and messaging for the intermediate and long terms.

Let's consider the example of a town that's been flooded by a rising river. The short-term focus will be on getting people into shelters and providing care; your mission as a communicator is to spread the word as widely as possible about how people can get out of harm's way and access those services.

In the weeks following, the emphasis will be on restoring infrastructure and critical services like water, sewers, and power. Your communications team can be sharing stories of successes and survival and information about timelines and the precise steps families need to take to get housing.

In the months to come, the focus will shift to creating permanent solutions for proactively dealing with flood danger and guidelines for rebuilding homes so they're safe the next time there's flooding. This is the most difficult phase for a communicator, because there's much less of a sense of urgency and people aren't paying as close attention as they once did. You can emphasize the communal vision for what the town will look like once rebuilt in full and how people can get involved in the planning process.

Juggling Legal Advice

In a significant crisis, your organization's leadership should be listening closely to their attorney's advice. Legal advice should almost always be followed—but sometimes that counsel will conflict with your best practices for communications. Deciding how to move forward in this case is a balancing act involving decisions that only your leadership can make.

As a PR professional, you need to work closely with your organization's attorneys in developing your crisis communications plan. Getting early buy-in and input into the plan's development can help smooth over many issues down the road. Take time to understand their concerns and the big-picture implications for your agency in a range of potential situations. Most attorneys are simply intent on limiting your legal exposure and risk. That doesn't mean they're always right—but it does make things easier when you need to compromise.

I once worked with a government attorney who wanted reporters to submit all questions in writing—using the official system for requesting public records, which then involved a complicated and convoluted weeks-long process of searching and legal review. The attorney's twisted logic was that since all information we would give to the reporters came from our records in some way, that process should naturally apply. That was a bizarre way to think about public relations and would have completely cut the knees out from under all government agencies that tried to engage the media. Thankfully, I was able to explain the inevitable impact of his theory to our leadership, and commonsense PR prevailed.

Admitting Mistakes

It's human nature to not want to admit a mistake. It can feel as though doing so will only lead to embarrassment and negative consequences of all sorts. In a crisis that's playing out in the media, it can also mean public humiliation. There can be legal ramifications to acknowledging that your organization or an individual erred. But admitting error is often the right thing to do—from both an ethical perspective, which I'll leave to the philosophy majors, and a public-relations standpoint.

Crafting an apology is an art in itself. The best way is to keep it simple and sincere, using straightforward language that pulls no punches and doesn't try to hide behind passive phrasing, jargon, or legal gibberish. Ripping the bandage off quickly leads to better results.

A three-step system usually works best: admitting the mistake, apologizing for it, and explaining how you're making improvements or changes.

We made a mistake at [PROBLEM].
We're sorry for how this mistake affected [PEOPLE].
We are working to do better and taking immediate action to [CHANGE].

What's in Your Kit?

Chances are very good that a crisis may take you away from your office for a while—to a jobsite, a partner agency, or a disaster location. You need to be ready to work off-site for both short periods and extended stays, and be fully ready to do whatever needs to be done remotely—from writing news releases to talking on-camera. That's where your crisis kit, also known as a "go bag," becomes essential. Think creatively about what you need to have on hand, including items such as:

- ☐ complete change of clothes, for both the field and on-camera situations
- ☐ sturdy, practical, comfortable shoes
- ☐ hooded rain jacket or poncho
- ☐ laptop computer with Wi-Fi hot spot
- ☐ surge protector
- ☐ extension cord
- ☐ key documents, images, and video assets, in hard copy and saved to your hard drive, a flash drive, and *also* a cloud service
- ☐ cell phone charger and portable battery or external power source
- ☐ notebooks, pens, folders, and other such supplies
- ☐ preprinted signage with your organization's logo, URL, and phone number
- ☐ mints and gum
- ☐ media contact list, printed
- ☐ organizational contact list, printed
- ☐ passwords for social media accounts
- ☐ camera with extra batteries and charger
- ☐ flashlight and batteries

- [ ] personal medical supplies (prescriptions, contact lens solutions, etc.)
- [ ] personal toiletries
- [ ] first aid kit
- [ ] extra masks and hand sanitizer
- [ ] cash for emergencies
- [ ] sleeping bag
- [ ] bottled water
- [ ] shelf-stable snacks, such as protein bars, hard candies, fig bars, fruit leathers, nuts, etc.

Note that all your key documents should be available in hard copy and in multiple digital locations. Never rely on just one storage location. Your flash drive could become crushed, your hard drive could be corrupted, and your cloud storage service may be unavailable if you don't have an internet connection. This applies to all your pre-written material—holding statements, news releases, talking points, and social media posts, in addition to contact lists for the media and your key organization staff.

When you upload your documents to a cloud service, make sure they're also available on your mobile device offline. Google Docs has an excellent feature that allows this. I've used items stored in the cloud to write news releases while sitting in a parking lot and sent out full releases from the site of a news conference without waiting until I made it back to the office. In a pinch during a crisis, you may find yourself at a remote site without internet access but needing to send out an alert. Planning ahead will make things much easier.

THE TAKEAWAY

Managing crisis communications is almost as important as managing the actual crisis itself. Crises have a way of burning themselves into our memories, and people will long remember how your organization presented itself and talked.

The resources you should have at hand include:

- a well-developed crisis communications plan
- the trust, confidence, and support of your leadership
- relationships with local partners and responders
- ideas from training conferences and webinars
- a packed "go kit" with all the physical items and documents you need

Above all: Don't panic. Calm your mind. Fear feeds on itself and will definitely show through to your audiences.

— 10 —

AMPLIFYING THE MESSAGE

Smithville

Bob Guthrie is president of the Smithville Volunteer Fire Company, coordinating all the behind-the-scenes work that keeps the fire-fighters going. On the communications front, he produces a steady volume of news releases about trainings, certifications, equipment, and new projects that keeps his team busy. But while much of his audience is on social media, he doesn't have a lot of time to write brand-new posts. And even though fundraising is a major goal for the company, he feels overwhelmed by the idea of having to write appeal letters and grant applications.

Writing a press release, getting it approved, building your media list, and sending it off into the ether with a click leaves you with a very satisfied feeling.

But it isn't the end of your job—it's just the beginning.

Today, public-relations work is intimately tied in with social media, websites, newsletters, thought leadership, and content marketing, especially at smaller or more local organizations or businesses.

You may be responsible for storytelling for your entire organization, and that involves a lot of details that didn't exist 10 or even 5 years ago.

Here's how you can edit, retool, and repurpose some basic content—like in a news release—for other types of content and channels as well.

Thinking Beyond the Media

A properly crafted news release is just the starting point. As a way to attract the media's attention and get that release published as its own story, it's an excellent tool. But it's not the end goal by any means.

It's likely that there are more people in your region on social media than reading the weekly newspaper. That's just a fact of declining print circulation combined with virtually ubiquitous social media access. If you really want to maximize the number of people who will see your story, you must be thinking more creatively and planning to do more than just getting reporters to do interviews.

You have to take control of your own story on your own turf. And that requires a little bit more creativity and certainly more time than just firing out a news release to a media contact list.

If you're hired for a professional role in communications these days, the job description will almost certainly include social media, website content, developing thought leadership pieces, and content marketing among the responsibilities. It's relatively rare for a local or smaller organization to have separate people handling each of those duties. If you're a small-business owner who's been trying to do all this yourself, you already know how difficult it can be to develop new content for all these different platforms. It's almost certainly overwhelming and confusing.

The good news is that it doesn't have to be. Here's how to make that happen.

A Treasure Trove

What marketing pros call "content marketing," you can call a collection of great riches. That 400-word news release you've already created and whatever photos you've got available can be mined for new content for weeks to come, making your life simpler and easier. You can easily rework and reshape your releases into website copy, social media posts, newsletter articles, and op-ed columns.

I'm a big believer in being efficient and not reinventing the wheel. If I've described a process or a program well once for a website, I don't need to sweat over doing it again using different words for a newsletter. At some point, all I'd be doing is using a thesaurus to find new synonyms for the same words, which doesn't help anyone. If your organization has the copyright and owns the words, you can use them however you want. Most of your audience isn't going to be tracking your language and complaining that you used the same sentence in a brochure and in a Facebook post.

Website Copy

You probably already have a website in place for your business or organization. (If you don't, you need one!) It's a general rule of website content and online marketing that your site should not remain static. Repeat visitors need something new to look at. Casual searchers need new material to ping in their web searches. People seeking educational or how-to information, news about your industry, or expertise on a particular topic need someplace to go.

Adding a news section to your website is a good way to repurpose your news releases *and* keep your latest information and programs in front of your most loyal audience. You can simply upload them with minimal editing and rewriting, remembering that your audience has now shifted from a newspaper reader or TV news viewer to someone coming across the article weeks or months later. I will often remove any date or time reference in the story, so that doesn't create a jarring sensation for the reader. Make sure that your headline is optimized for your website's format or theme and doesn't wrap around or overlay onto images accidentally.

Social Media

Of course, you can simply share your news releases on social media, once you remove the contact information and all the media-oriented formatting. Copying and pasting, while uploading an image or URL, is certainly the fastest way of reaching your social audience. But it's not the best way. Here are some examples of how to repurpose your story on social:

> **PULL QUOTE** Take the best quotations in the story—ones that can stand on their own without any introduction or explanation—and create social images featuring the quotes. (Be sure to include the quote itself in the text of the post to allow people using screen-reader devices to hear them.)

> **TEASER** Write a short summary of the story for your social platform—one or two sentences maximum—setting up the problem that gets solved in your story. Include a short teaser phrase and the URL, like: "Learn about how Smithville, Inc., solved the client's programming challenges here." The goal is to whet their appetite and funnel them to your website.

> **DATA POINT** Extract a key point of data that's highlighted in your release, like how you serve 5,000 children each month in an after-school program, or how 84 percent of your martial arts academy students earned at least two new belts last year. Create a social image with the data point big and bold, with text underneath detailing what it's about.

> **EXPLAINER** Use the nut graf (see Chapter 4) from your release to explain a key element of your program or product to your audience.

DID YOU KNOW? Pull any interesting, little-known, or startling fact from the story to showcase in a "Did You Know?" format: "Did you know that Smithville, Inc., was founded as a horseshoe manufacturing operation in 1824? Today we're Ohio's largest custom tire manufacturer, continuing our mission of keeping the Buckeye State running."

Remember that every platform has different technical and image specifications, so one size very rarely fits all. You'll have to do some customization and editing for each one—but having a baseline of source material to draw from will make your work much easier and simpler.

Smithville ――――――――――――――――――――――――――――――

IN ACTION: To increase his fire company's reach, Bob Guthrie started using the stories in his news releases as a base for social media posts. On Instagram, he highlighted a photo from a training session of firefighters trying on new protective gear. On Facebook, he did a light rewrite of a news release to create a story about a fundraiser for a new piece of ambulance equipment that would save lives. And to craft the annual appeal letter to local residents, he turned a six-month-old release about the dramatic rescue of a family from their burning apartment into a three-paragraph narrative that attracted attention and increased donations by 12 percent.

Newsletter Items

An email newsletter is another great tool in your marketing toolbox, allowing you to share information and insights with your current customers or clients, prospects, and other people who have expressed an interest in your organization. Your news release can be easily adapted and edited to fit a content gap in your newsletter, usually with very little editing. The headline will take the most work, especially if you want to use it as a subject line. Sometimes you can break the news release into various parts—a main story, a photo, a pull quote, and a data highlight—that can even fill the entire newsletter.

Remember that shorter is generally better with newsletters. You want to provide enough material that your reader is interested and gains something valuable, but not so much that they're just scrolling . . . and scrolling . . . and scrolling. Many readers today are viewing newsletters on their smartphone screens, so a few paragraphs can look like a really dense wall of text.

Infographics

An infographic is a way of presenting data and information that's easy to understand at a glance. Charts and graphs are common types, typically featuring numbers and statistics, but also useful are timelines, lists, maps, and processes or steps. You can use them on websites and social media, in e-newsletters, and in print publications such as annual reports, posters, or fundraising appeals. There are lots of templates available online that you can modify with the right software or use as inspiration, so you don't have to build from scratch.

What type of information is featured in your news release? Your story about nonprofit programs expanding to a new area could be represented visually as a map. If your business is launching a new e-commerce site, you can create a process flowchart showing how simple it is to order. The changes to your school's admissions process can be shown as a timeline to explain exactly how it will be implemented.

Photographs and Video Clips

Good-quality photos are worth their weight in gold. Photos of events, programs, staff, and products, as well as historical images, can provide a long line of posts and content for social media, newsletters, and reports. Video can be extremely powerful in creating a narrative with appeal on multiple platforms. For both of these mediums, think back to how we discussed event planning: Make sure you have more than just images or footage of a person in a suit standing behind a lectern.

Go behind the scenes, gather material in real-world environments, get close-ups, and shoot from the top of the bleachers rather than on the field.

Having a high-quality image and video archive will pay huge dividends later—but only if you can find what you need when you need it. Develop a simple organizational system that outsiders (or your successor) can easily understand. Tag or label your files and folders with events, locations, and dates. Copy commonly used files into a quick-reference folder. For organizations with a truly large volume of material, look into a digital asset management system that will more easily let you tag and search for your files.

White Papers

A white paper is a marketing or educational tool with an awful name— "white paper" just sounds extremely bland and completely dry. In reality, a well-done white paper can be highly informative and help tell your story to a broader audience, while reinforcing your organization's authority as an influencer.

White papers should be based on original insights or research that helps solve a problem for your core audience. Incorporate graphics and charts to explain complex topics. Stories drawn from news releases can make for excellent scene-setters and problem statements.

Annual Reports

Unless your organization is truly stodgy and utterly old-fashioned, chances are good that your leadership will want to make its annual report attractive and appealing, reinventing what came before. I once filled several pages of an agency's report with stories rewritten from news releases and social media posts. There was no need to reinvent the wheel.

Newspaper Columns

Skimming through your local newspaper week after week, you'll likely find several columns not written by the news staff but by outside contributors. These are typically called op-ed columns or opinion columns, shared by local leaders, business owners, and nonprofit leaders to draw attention to a particular topic. Despite their name, op-eds aren't always about sharing opinions or debating an issue. A good op-ed column can highlight your recent accomplishments, profile an outstanding staff member, or showcase an event and its impact. You just have to tell a story with a bit of a news hook; many columns use a national observance like Mental Illness Awareness Week or National Manufacturing Day to create some news value. Rather than a straight news story (remember Chapter 4), columns are usually written from an "I" or "we" perspective.

If your news release doesn't get covered by the media, following up with an op-ed column highlighting the issue can be an excellent alternative that will still get some readers to pay attention. And even if your topic *did* get some news attention, you can always submit a column a few weeks later highlighting a particular angle that the media didn't cover.

Your Own Media Channels

Amy Higgins, whom we met in Chapter 7, created her own "news outlets" for her Ohio school district. She built a newspaper that goes to every home in the city (circulation 25,000), called the *Pioneer Press*; created regular videos on YouTube, known as PioneerTV; and even launched a podcast. All the content is interconnected, across platforms. "We work with everybody who does media, but we also are our own media," Higgins says. "If you're a one-man show and you're running your own thing, the best thing you can do is to find the way to tell your story without filters."

User-Generated Content

If you're a company or nonprofit that deals with the public, one of your best sources of content can be material that your users, clients, or customers send to you. Quotes about their experience with your services, photographs of your products in the real world, authentic stories about how you transformed their lives or solved their problem—those are all amazing ways to showcase what you do, with the power of a third-party testimonial. You can easily set up a form or uploader on your website to collect these submissions. Put a vetting process in place to ensure that they're real and not invented out of whole cloth.

THE TAKEAWAY

Long gone are the days when a public-relations team just had to churn out news releases and handle reporters' calls. Now, PR work often includes handling website content, social media, newsletters, opinion columns, and more.

Here are four ways to make that part of the job easier and repurpose that news release into dynamic content for your other communications channels:

- Use a powerful quote or story to make a nonprofit annual report pop.
- Take a focused angle and craft a column for your local newspapers.
- Create an organization podcast to share news and stories.
- Tease out data points and highlights for infographics and social posts.

Don't be afraid to repeat yourself, especially on social media. The majority of your followers don't see all your posts, so repetition is almost expected. And no one's going to complain about reading a great story twice.

"Just constantly telling the story"

Chrissy Kadleck found her way into public relations after a successful career as a newspaper journalist and freelance writer. She's applied those skills every day in her job as director of communications and employee engagement for Interlake Maritime Services, which owns the largest privately held US flag fleet on the Great Lakes, hauling cargo for industrial and other customers.

Her company's social media reach far surpasses what one might expect for a commercial shipping company. It reaches about 3 million people each month, with some 60,000 followers on Facebook alone. "It's really become a community that has a life of its own," Kadleck says. "Somebody has a father or an uncle or a grandma or a grandpa that was on the boat or sailed on the Great Lakes or lived along the St. Clair River. These people have this deep love and affection for the boats and the industry."

Kadleck says running social media accounts for such a fiercely loyal audience is a serious job. "My goal is not to blow up your news feed with 10 pictures of boats that were around the Great Lakes on this particular day," she says. "I work hard to curate or create the best content for our followers. . . . I respect our followers. I think about, 'Is this something I want to see?' If I just post 10 things from a company each day, people are just going to unfollow me."

Food photos from aboard her company's vessels are a huge attraction. "People will go crazy," she says. "They love the food on board or the menus on our holidays." Kadleck also taps into a deep pool of enthusiasm for her company's ships, as fans ashore and crew members aboard both contribute stories and photos.

"One crew member shared how his daughter would always come down to one location when his boat passed by and she'd ring a bell and he would do a salute," she says. "We look for those kinds of things that humanize us and everybody can relate to."

So-called boat nerds on the shore capture a plethora of photos that Kadleck is eager to share, while giving proper credit to the photographers. "We're a 24/7 dynamic business that's pretty well documented by boat nerds all around the lakes," she explains. "They sit on the shore and take our pictures, and they love it when we share it on our pages. They get a lot of exposure."

She's conscious of the fact that some of those fans have a larger reach than she does. "Almost every person is their own media outlet now. Fans of our industry actually spread news more than I do for our company at times."

— 11 —

WHAT NOT TO DO

A large amount of public-relations work deals with relationships and, as such, people working in the PR world can easily and accidentally put a foot astray—in their mouth or stepping on someone's toes. This chapter identifies some of the most common pitfalls and missteps that you should avoid when navigating this field.

Don't Compare Yourself

There's always the instinct to look at what and how other businesses, schools, or nonprofits are doing, whether it's getting strong media attention or creating incredible social media content. It's OK to draw on inspiration from those examples, says Aaron Chusid, formerly with the Boy Scouts of America, but he advises: "Don't compare what you're doing to the organizations that have bigger budgets. You look at some new hospital that opens up and has a massive budget and can do all these things and what they're able to generate. If you're a local school district with a budget of 10 dollars, there's no way you're going to be able to match what they're doing."

Chusid suggests that you simply need to focus on what's in front of you. "Big PR firms or the big companies that have a larger PR department have more resources and generate more results. Know what your goals are, focus on those goals, and don't worry about what the bigger organizations are trying to do."

Don't Accuse Journalists of Bias

One of the worst things you can do is to get into a dispute with a journalist where you're accusing them of being biased against you. That's an ego war that no one will win. We all know that journalists bring personal biases to their work—that's just human nature, not anything diabolical. But if you openly make a statement like that, then that opens the doors to all-out war. Unless you have the receipts—and I'm talking about actual documentation, not just your perception or coincidences—you'll never get the reporter or their editor back on your side.

Don't Openly Play Favorites

It's all right to have your favorite reporters. I always enjoyed working with a handful of writers when I worked in state government—they were genuinely professional and a pleasure to deal with. But don't get friendly in public or openly grant them favors or access. In front of other reporters, that will create an impression that you're giving special treatment to one outlet over another. You can absolutely provide embargoed information to a select journalist or give them a behind-the-scenes tour. But don't embarrass that reporter or anger their colleagues by having those conversations in public.

And don't cross the line from common courtesy and friendliness into friendship. If you hang out with reporters in your downtime, word will get around and you'll lose your credibility—and theirs will be called into question too.

Don't Claim to Be an Advertiser or a Friend of the Publisher

Reporters and editors generally don't care about either of those things. At reputable, ethical outlets, there are walls between the advertising and business sides and the newsroom, as we saw in Chapter 5. Trying to find favor with a real journalist may even backfire if they think you're attempting to put a negative story on ice or pump up a puff piece—they may well pursue it even harder, or make sure other journalists know that you tried to buy your way on to the newscast.

Don't Overdo It

Be selective in your pitching and releases or eventually you may get a reputation as the boy who cried wolf. Sometimes it's unavoidable, and you just have to send out a lot of news at the same time; at the end of the academic year, many schools issue a barrage of news, with information on fourth-quarter honor roll, senior awards, and graduation ceremonies. But make that a once-a-year thing. Quality is almost always better than quantity.

To protect your organization's reputation, make sure that all your stories are high-quality ones. Don't waste anyone's time with news releases about an annual meeting that will interest no one except your members or a festival happening tomorrow. (Alternatives: Put out a summary of any actual action that took place at the meeting, and write a news release a few weeks ahead of the festival to attract attention.)

Don't Play Off-the-Record, On-the-Record Games

We talked about this earlier in Chapter 7, but it needs to be repeated here because it's so important. There's generally no need to talk with someone off the record—but if there is an advantage for you, make sure everyone knows the ground rules.

Journalist-turned-nonprofit-leader Kathie Klarriech says: "You just have to have an understanding from the beginning of what's on the record and what's off. You can't control what they ultimately write. But you can be very clear about what's on and off the record."

Don't Pitch to Someone Who Just Wrote an Identical Story

The worst time to propose a story about a new bagel shop opening up is right after a reporter has written a story about another new bagel shop opening up. You may think that reporter really likes to write about bagel shops—and she may—but eventually a subject reaches the point of saturation. A reporter who goes to their editor with a story almost the same as the one they just wrote is going to get laughed out of the newsroom.

As we noted in Chapter 5, timing is critical. Make sure you're reading, watching, and listening to your local media outlets to watch out for conflicts from similar stories.

Don't Use Jargon

Every industry, field, or profession has its own specialized language and terminology that improves communication within the sector—but also serves to keep out those not in the know. Jargon is fine to include in a story if you're pitching to a trade magazine or industry website; all the readers will understand precisely what is meant. In all other writing, you should work ruthlessly to cut it out.

This includes such words as synergy, best practice, impact, and mission critical—extremely common terms in the world of business, but which ordinary readers or viewers may not be familiar with. Remember that writing should be on a sixth- to eighth-grade level, so don't include terms that an eighth-grader wouldn't recognize or understand.

It's fairly simple to eliminate jargon—just cut it out entirely or replace it with a common, simple word or phrase. "Synergy" becomes simply "working together" or "cooperation." "Best practice" turns into "the right action." "Impact" becomes "effect." "Mission critical" becomes "essential" or just "critical."

One of the worst historical offenders when it came to using jargon has been the US government. Since 2010, the federal government has emphasized what's known as "plain language," offering many resources at plainlanguage.gov that can help you de-jargon your own writing. One of my favorite sections of the site contains examples of before-and-after language, showing just how easy it is to trim things down and make complex topics easily understandable.

Don't Pitch Junk

If your organization gets a reputation for sending non-newsworthy things, fewer people will be inclined to pay attention when you have something really good going on. Just because your business owner wants to send out a news release to the TV station about the hiring of a shift manager at your production facility doesn't mean you should. Send a photo and caption just to the local business newspaper or the Chamber of Commerce's newsletter instead. Be selective and careful.

Don't Be Too Precious

Bruce Bishop, chief photographer for an Ohio newspaper, cautions agencies and businesses not to hold their news too closely. "We get too many requests to cover something where the topic isn't being released before the meeting," he says. "It's incredibly frustrating playing the mystery game. Ninety percent of the time, the media contact thinks their big secret is an epic release, and we see it as nothing worth the dog and pony show."

Instead, he advises, if something really can't be put out before a certain date—if your franchisee is restricting the information, or if you're working with another school on a special project—then put it out under an embargo, as we discussed in Chapter 5. Keep in mind that not everyone will abide by an embargo, particularly if they haven't agreed to it first.

Don't Fall for Fast-Talking Hype Artists

There's a racket for everything, it seems—even public relations. I first encountered one particular grift close to a decade ago. It works like this: A production company of dubious ethics will buy airtime on a cable news channel or in-flight entertainment lineup and produce a show that looks a lot like a traditional news program. There's a studio, a celebrity or former journalist doing the interviews, and a lineup of nonprofit leaders and business executives traipsing through for their moment in the spotlight.

The difference between these operations and real journalism is that this arrangement is pay-for-play, which real reporters and editors don't do. They want you to pay a few thousand dollars for the opportunity to be interviewed and featured on their program.

These tricksters rely on local and regional organizations not knowing that real media outlets don't require payment for an interview. They're banking on people getting starry-eyed at the prospect of being on the set with a D-list celebrity and getting their time in the sun.

I worked for our state agriculture agency when I got this pitch, and recall that their ask was around $6,000 for a half hour of airtime. That would have been a significant chunk of money to us—in fact, it would probably have been cheaper for us just to book the airtime for ourselves as an ad.

If you get a call like this, ignore it—or better yet, tell them to stuff it.

I'll repeat again: You don't pay to get covered by the press.

Don't Assume They Know Your Business

When working with the average local news reporter, the odds are good that they had *maybe* a few minutes to do a web search about your organization and that they don't have a deep background—or any background—in the subject they're asking questions about. If you're lucky, a reporter may be covering your sector as a particular beat and may be able to ask intelligent, deep questions. But then again, they might not.

Chrissy Kadleck (from Chapter 10), who works in the highly technical shipping industry, says: "Don't assume they understand your industry or bring any additional knowledge. Use the phrase, 'I'm not sure if you're aware,' or 'Most people find it fascinating to know this...' It's a nice way to pivot and do your talking points, just a nicer way to deal with people."

Don't Assume They're Sticklers for the Details

Some reporters are good at nailing down the specifics of a story. They ask for spellings, definitions, clarifications. Others may be more focused on the broad themes of the narrative and not pay much attention to those pesky details. Kadleck suggests preparing by writing down those details as much as you can.

"The more that you give them in writing—titles, names, exact way things should appear—the better chance that there won't be corrections or things that you have to follow up on," she says. "I just try to eliminate the room for error whenever possible, but not be controlling. I really don't like people to feel like they're being controlled by a PR person."

Don't Leave Them Hanging

If you promise to get back in touch with a reporter, or if you have to look information up, make sure you do it promptly, says school district communications leader Amy Higgins. "They will do their story with or without you," she advises. "You're better off to provide them with the information they're seeking so they don't go out and find it somewhere else that may not be accurate."

Don't Be a Jerk

Just as you remember journalists who may be rude or dismissive, journalists definitely remember people they deal with who are aggressive, antagonistic, or unhelpful. "Give them what they want, be helpful," says Higgins. "Try to give them something that helps them with their job. . . . Even if it's more work for you, it helps you later because they remember that. In crisis situations, it's nice to have friends. It's nice to have people who believe what you're saying and want to work with you."

Kadleck agrees, saying, "I'll always follow up with people: 'How did the interview go with so-and-so? Did you have any additional questions? I can send you some photos.' I focus very much on being a helper to get the story published and help it along, and make their job easier."

Don't Duel with the Media

There's an old saying in PR: Don't pick a fight with someone who buys ink by the barrel. Chusid, who worked in the rough-and-tumble Washington, DC, media market, has this advice: "Don't try to impress anyone. A reporter from the *Washington Post* has spent much more time breaking much tougher sources than me. I gain nothing by trying to prove that I can outsmart them or joust with them or anything like that. . . . Even if you 'win,' you have nothing to gain. . . . Just stick to your message, stick to your mission, and achieve what you're trying to achieve."

— 12 —

TEAMWORK TIPS AND CAREER ADVICE

You may work for an organization that has a communications or PR team. If so, congratulations! It's a lot of stress to be a one-person shop, with your fingers dabbling in everything but never having enough time to concentrate on one or two major tasks.

When you become part of a team, you can divide the duties many different ways. You may choose to have one person handling social media and the website, another who spends their time writing news releases and web copy and editing others' work, another person who focuses on graphic design for print and digital platforms, and a fourth who handles media relations. You could have people who concentrate on event coordination, business-to-business (B2B) marketing, or SEO. The exact division of duties will depend on your needs as an organization or business.

You'll soon discover that communication *inside* your communications team is even more important than outside it. A good team needs to coordinate messaging and timing across platforms and events, so that what you put out on social media matches what your CEO is saying at a news conference, all of which is backed up by the content on your website. That requires planning and leadership from a good manager with a strategic eye.

If you're new to an organization, you'll need an in-depth under-standing of how the entire structure operates. Plan to spend your first few weeks getting to know the other departments and divisions through both informal and formal methods—interviews, tours, casual conversations over lunch. Schedule one-on-ones with the senior staff to understand their biggest challenges in PR and communications. Talk with the subject-matter experts to wrap your head around why they do certain things in a particular way. Offer to help with simple side projects that are in your wheelhouse—that will help build good-will up and down the organization chart.

You may find that you were hired to create a PR structure from nothing. That's almost freeing, in a way, because there will be a lot of low-hanging fruit—simple things you can do to get instant results. I was tapped once to get positive publicity for an employer that hadn't had much in recent years. I spent a lot of my time on the job per-suading my coworkers of the value of getting good stories in the local newspapers. Once the first article got picked up, it became easier to get the time and resources needed to do my job. Keep showcasing those successes to continue getting buy-in across the company.

If your organization considers you a low-level functionary, just carrying out requests from higher up the chain of command, you need to gradually, strategically, and diplomatically make the case that PR is a senior staff role that needs connections to the highest levels of the organization. Communications work isn't like running an on-demand delivery service; it should be part of a strategic function. Changing that mindset may take some time, unless the C-suite is invested in making PR a success. But your goal should be to get a seat at the table where the decisions are made. Communications should be an integral part of your business or organization's overall strategy and not just farmed out at the last minute.

Exploring a Long-Term Career

If you're interested in a career in PR, communications, or marketing, there are many pathways and options open to you. While career choices in journalism have shrunk along with the industry, the opposite is true in the communications arena. Job growth in the public-relations field is projected to grow by 11 percent through 2030, according to the US Bureau of Labor Statistics. There will be about 5,400 openings each year for journalists and 29,200 openings in PR.

I'm a firm believer that the best public-relations people are those who have prior professional experience in journalism. If you can get that background early—even if it's working on a college newspaper or freelancing for your local weekly covering town council meetings—it will be a great help in your future PR work. You'll understand more about how reporters and editors think, the types of stories they're interested in, and how deadlines and timing come into play in sometimes unexpected ways.

When on the job search, cast a wide net. Titles in this field can vary widely from business to business and even sector to sector. For example, the title "public information officer" is often used in education and law enforcement, but it is generally not found in the corporate world. You'll find jobs posted under public relations, to be sure, but also under community relations, media relations, corporate communications, public information, marketing and communications . . . and the list goes on.

Once you have some years under your belt, you may want to explore gaining additional certifications or pursuing education. You don't need a specific degree to work in public relations, but PRSA does offer the Accredited in Public Relations credential, or APR. There are specialized certifications for digital marketing and particular tools and platforms, such as HubSpot or Google Analytics. And in some industry sectors, earning an MBA or other advanced degree might be useful for advancement.

Application Advice

For some time now, I've been curating and maintaining a weekly list of jobs in the marketing and communications field in my home state of Delaware. We have a relatively small community of PR professionals in the state, so it's just a free resource to help friends and coworkers in their job hunts. I've noticed a few trends develop over the time that I've been doing this; here's my best advice on how to stand out from the crowd when applying, based on these observations.

First, you should **have a portfolio of work samples prepared** to send off. Many job postings don't ask for your portfolio right off the bat, but you should be ready to submit or attach work samples to your application up-front anyway. Your portfolio should be simple and straightforward, saved as a complete PDF with everything in one file. You don't necessarily need an online portfolio for an application; most companies are going to want a PDF anyway. When you're on the job, save copies or screenshots of major work that you're proud of in your personal files. Once you leave, you can't count on websites or social media platforms remaining active.

Second, **focus your résumé on accomplishments, not job duties**. Spend a little time each week digging into your website analytics, documenting the news coverage you've achieved, or breaking down your social media statistics. Quantify the number of media events you've organized, attendance increases at workshops you've promoted, the volume of talking points you've written, and any efficiencies you've been responsible for. Write those numbers down and take them with you when you leave so you have a record for your future reference. Numbers speak much more loudly than words to hiring managers.

Third, **broaden your experience beyond your job**. If you have the time, do some freelance writing on the side that can serve to showcase your skills and position you as an expert. I love summer camps—my first book was a history of a local camp—and have contributed several how-to articles on communications and marketing to magazines serving the summer camp industry. Those are great types of clips to have on your résumé and LinkedIn profile.

Build Your Network

Once you get settled, find an organization to join that will help you build your PR network. In many metro areas, there are local chapters of the Public Relations Society of America. There may also be local press associations that welcome other communications professionals as members. If you work in the nonprofit field, ask your state non-profit alliance if it can help organize a communications affinity group for its members. Go to events, participate in fundraisers, enter awards contests, and ask lots of questions. The more people you know in your area, the greater your support network will be when you run into problems or need assistance in a crisis.

There may also be national groups for your specific industry that you can join. Schools have access to the National School Public Relations Association, for example. When I worked for a state agriculture agency, I was a member and officer of the Communications Officers of State Departments of Agriculture, or COSDA—a fairly niche organization, certainly, but one with a huge professional impact in the field. We'd get together once a year for training, presentations, professional development, and networking, and any member could call on the group for assistance throughout the rest of the year.

Find a Mentor

Finding a trusted advisor early on can do your career a great deal of good. In my first journalism job, I was a kid who'd worked on a weekly campus newspaper at a tiny college in Ohio; I didn't know much. For my very first assignment, I nodded sagely at what the editor told me, then emailed a college friend at the first opportunity: "How many words are in a column inch?" Later, I was lucky enough to have three great bosses there who took the time to show me the ropes and teach me about professional standards.

It's difficult to find that kind of mentor when you're the only person doing communications at a local nonprofit, school system, or small business. That doesn't mean those are bad places to work—on the contrary, they can be excellent employers that offer a lot of creative freedom. There's just no formal structure in place for your professional development and growth.

If you're in that situation, you can still find a mentor in your field. Connect with your local chapter of the Public Relations Society of America, with other larger school districts, with your local nonprofit association, or with a larger state agency that has a full communications team. They'll be able to point you in the right direction. LinkedIn is also a good resource for finding people in your field nearby; look for second- and third-level connections who freely share advice and perspectives on the job. You want to look for someone who has at least 5 years of professional experience, preferably 10 or 15. A mid-level manager or deputy director would be perfect—they're not going to be as tied up as the top person, but they will have plenty of insights and advice to share.

The Big Transition

If you're a journalist who's interested in moving into PR, then you already have half the skills you need—and you can learn the other half quickly. Your challenge will be persuading hiring managers that an ex-journalist can be an effective spokesperson and communications coordinator. Some PR managers and companies have a bizarre preference for hiring only people with public-relations degrees or experience working in a PR agency; they refuse to look at the résumés of people who've been editing and writing stories from their pitches for years. That's just their loss!

When I moved from newspaper reporting to PR, I argued that I knew public relations already—just from the other side of the fence. I could write quickly, edit efficiently, design publications. I knew what reporters wanted and needed, because I'd been one for the prior five years. That helped convince them to give me a try.

Journalists today have access to a wealth of internal online audience metrics on their articles and columns that was kept closely held when I last worked in a newsroom. Without sharing confidential company information, you can still highlight how your articles were read 10 percent more than other reporters' or how your rewrites of headlines increased their viewership by 18 percent on average. You can easily track and quantify the volume of stories written, photos taken, or articles edited. Showing those metrics will also tell a hiring manager that you are focused on measurable results and will fit in well with a data-driven team.

FINAL WORDS

In your leadership role in a business, nonprofit, school, or government position, you may feel like there's no flexibility to teach yourself and learn as you go.

But if you can use online tips and videos to learn how to install a refrigerator, rewire an outlet, or hook up a washer, then you can do the same thing on the job. The do-it-yourself approach is all about learning independently from authoritative sources, going step by step to create a plan, and then applying what you've learned to real life.

I hope that this book has opened your eyes to what's possible in getting solid local media attention—and using that to advance your organization's strategic objectives.

You've learned how to communicate in a crisis, how to craft clear and concise statements, and how to excel in on-camera interviews. You've gotten insider insights on connecting with reporters, handling difficult media situations, developing your story, and creating content to expand your audience.

Reporters, editors, and producers today have an exceedingly tough job. Your job, trying to get their attention, is even more difficult. This book has shown you the path to success.

Now go out there and tell your stories.

—Dan Shortridge

p.s. I'd love to hear about your successes using the techniques and advice in this book. Please visit danshortridge.com and send me a note.

APPENDIX
SAMPLES AND TEMPLATES

The exact format of a news release or statement matters far less than the content. To be sure, there are certain elements that you must include—a headline, a contact name, phone number, and email are always critical. But don't bother yourself with whether the contact details should be on the right side of the page or the left side, or how large the headline needs to be, for example. That's all formatting and frippery. Just make sure your subject line, headline, and story are sound, and you've done 95 percent of what you need to do.

MEDIA ADVISORY

Advisories are simple alerts to inform or remind reporters, editors, and producers of a media event coming up. They're generally not intended for public consumption. Send an advance release or calendar item for events geared toward the general readership or viewership. An advisory should be short, sweet, and formatted for easy reading and quick comprehension by a busy editor.

SAMPLE

FOR PLANNING PURPOSES

Contact: Zeta Smith, 555-555-5555 or zetasmith@emailaddress.com

MEDIA ADVISORY

Governor Smith to announce new state early literacy program and $5M grant to Smithville Youth Foundation

WHAT:

Governor Jane Smith will unveil a new state initiative to promote early literacy and a $5 million grant to the Smithville Youth Foundation to run the program, in coordination with the state Division of Libraries. The new program will help an estimated 50,000 young children start reading earlier.

WHO:

Governor Jane Smith
Pete Smith, state libraries director
Precious Jones-Smith, president, Smithville Youth Foundation
Roger Smith, early literacy coach
Frances Smith, parent

WHEN:

10–10:45 A.M.
Tuesday, March 17

WHERE:

Smithville Youth Foundation, 555 Smith Road, Smithville, NY
Livestreamed on the Smithville Youth Foundation website,
siteaddresshere.com

RSVP / CONTACT:

Zeta Smith, 555-555-5555 or zetasmith@emailaddress.com.
The day of the event, contact Alpha Smith, 555-555-5555

TEMPLATE

FOR PLANNING PURPOSES

Contact: Person's name, phone number with area code, and email address

MEDIA ADVISORY

Headline goes here, directly stating what will happen and the impact

WHAT:

A summary line goes here recapping and providing more detail than in the headline. Include dollar amounts, number of people affected, and any other details you have at hand.

WHO:

Put the names of the speakers and other major attendees here. Include only the people who are guaranteed and confirmed. Highlight any real people you have confirmed.

WHEN:

The time, day of the week, and the date go here.

WHERE:

Include the exact location and any directions that attendees might need to know here. Link to exact directions if you are able. Include information on where to park, signage, and landmarks. If it's being livestreamed or is a virtual event, include a URL or details on how to get the meeting link.

RSVP / CONTACT:

Include contact information for reporters to RSVP and, if needed, a different day-of-event contact as well.

NEWS RELEASE—EVENT PREVIEW

This type of news release is designed to increase public awareness of an upcoming public event—for example, a community fair, a school open house, or a training session. Local media outlets are very likely to simply run your story verbatim rather than write their own, unless it's a certifiable big deal.

SAMPLE

NEWS RELEASE
SMITHVILLE SCHOOL DISTRICT

October 24, 2021

Contact: Person's name, phone number (with area code), and email address

Families can learn about Smithville Elementary School programs at November 5 open house

More than 700 eligible families across Smithville County interested in learning about Smithville Elementary School programs are invited to its annual open house on Saturday, November 5.

Students can tour classrooms, meet their future teachers, play games, and meet current students. Parents can talk with teachers, hear from a panel of current parents, and learn about educational technology and next school year's plans.

"We hope that all our families can enjoy the day and learn more about what their children will be learning and experiencing next year," said Smithville Elementary Principal Joseph Meyer.

Doors will open at 9 a.m., with an optional presentation for new Smithville-area families at 9:30 a.m. Tours begin at 9:15 a.m. and run every 30 minutes. The open house will run until 12:30 p.m.

Parents can register their children on-site for next year at the open house, pick up paperwork to take home and mail back, or log on to smithvilleschoolswebsite.com to register online.

The school is located at 555 Smithville Avenue, Smithville, NY. Plenty of on-site parking is available; follow the signs to the main entrance from the parking lot. For more information, call the school office at 555-555-5555.

NEWS RELEASE
SMITHVILLE SCHOOL DISTRICT

Date of Release Goes Here

Contact: Person's name, phone number (with area code), and email address

Headline goes here, with enough information to grab someone's attention; include the date of event

The lead paragraph here includes all the basic information of who, what, when, where, why, and how. Because this is an event preview, make sure to include the day of week and date.

The second paragraph provides more details about what will be happening at the event and who can participate. Will there be presentations, interactive activities, panels, Q&As, tours? Are there age limits? Will there be special speakers who will be known to the public?

"The third paragraph, here, should be a quote about the event, reinforcing the key points above," said Organizer's Name and Title.

The fourth paragraph needs to have details about the timing, schedule, or other arrangements. Provide enough information so attendees can figure out their plans without having to call or check your website.

The fifth paragraph can feature other information that people need to know about the event, the sponsor, or the procedures or protocols.

The sixth paragraph should include the full address, information on parking or directions, and public contact information.

NEWS RELEASE—HARD NEWS

A hard-news release is the most common type that you'll be writing. They are meant to be complete stories announcing your basic news: new funding, new programs, business start-ups, expansions, etc.

SAMPLE

NEWS RELEASE
SMITHVILLE YOUTH FOUNDATION

October 24, 2021

Contact: Person's name, phone number (with area code), and email address

New summer teen jobs program to launch in Smithville

To help local teenagers find their first job, about 50 area businesses will join forces in a new summer jobs program, the Smithville Youth Foundation announced Tuesday.

About 150 teenagers will be accepted into the program to work at jobs ranging from retail clerk to lifeguard, camp counselor to automotive tech, Foundation President Geraldine Smith said.

"It's tough for teenagers to land their first job without any experience," she said. "We're extending a helping hand and providing a structure and support to these first-time job seekers."

The new initiative is supported with funds from the state Department of Labor. State Senator Adam Clayton Smith, who pushed for the funding in the last legislative session, said the new initiative is a win-win for employers and teenagers alike.

"Our business community needs these entry-level workers to provide a steady stream of talent, creating a pipeline to fill future openings," he said. "Teenagers need extra support to fine-tune their applications and get help preparing for interviews."

The program will begin accepting applications in January and the new hires will start working in May after a mandatory two-day paid onboarding workshop to cover various soft skills, the Foundation's Smith said. Applications will be accepted at smithvilleyouthfoundationwebsite.com or available from high school guidance offices.

Additional employers are still being sought to match with potential employees. For information, contact the Foundation at 555-555-5555.

TEMPLATE

NEWS RELEASE
[YOUR ORGANIZATION]

Date of Release Goes Here

Contact: Person's name, phone number (with area code), and email address

Headline goes here, direct and simple; don't clutter it

The lead sentence or paragraph breaks the story down to its simplest possible terms, remembering the who, what, where, when, why, and how. The attribution—who is doing this or who said it—is also important.

The second paragraph will provide more details about the news, including numbers, deadlines, goals, etc. It can stand on its own or be attributed to the person delivering your first quote.

"The first quote, located here, can offer a quotable quip while providing context or appealing to the target audience," said First Speaker, Job Title. "The second part of the first quote can go here elaborating on the first parts."

The fourth paragraph can get into more details about the news announcement, such as the funding, how the project is being managed, and key supporters. It can even lead into a quote by your second speaker.

"The second quote, here, is optional, but can be an opportunity to recognize a funding partner, VIP, or other leader," said Second Speaker, Job Title. "The quotes should make points that complement but do not duplicate the first speaker's. The second part of this quote can go here elaborating on the first parts."

The sixth, seventh, and eighth paragraphs should fill in any other details about the news announcement, such as deadlines, application periods, details of how it will roll out, and how to apply or get involved. Program contact information and names should go here, along with the website link.

NEWS RELEASE—STAFF HIGHLIGHTS

Some changes in staff are bigger news than others; the hiring of a nonprofit director is more important than a middle manager promotion, for example. But each may get some news coverage. Back in Chapter 3, we discussed "People in Business" columns in many local newspapers that round up recent staff hirings, accomplishments, and promotions. Help all your team members get the recognition they deserve by showcasing their accomplishments to the local media.

SAMPLE

NEWS RELEASE
SMITHVILLE CONSULTING

October 24, 2021

Contact: Person's name, phone number (with area code), and email address

Smith named CEO of Smithville Consulting, Jones promoted to CFO

Industry veteran Jane Smith has been named the new CEO of Smithville Consulting and will succeed Elwood Smith-Jones in the role starting January 1, the firm's board of directors announced Tuesday.

"We are looking forward to having Jane Smith's talented leadership to steer the company in the right direction," said board President Arnie Smith. "We cannot say enough about the service and dedication of Elwood Smith-Jones and wish him all the best in his pending retirement."

Most recently CEO of Bakerville Consulting, Smith has spent the last 25 years in management consulting, helping clients from the Fortune 500 to Main Street. She is a noted public speaker and author of the book How It's Done: Dynamic Management Consulting for the 22nd Century. She holds an MBA from Smithville University and a bachelor's degree in economics from Smithville College.

Smith-Jones, CEO of Smithville Consulting for the last decade, will assume an emeritus role as senior advisor beginning January 1 to assist with the transition and will enter retirement on July 1. Before joining the firm, Smith-Jones was a vice president at Underwater Enterprises handling mergers and acquisitions. He holds a master's degree in horticulture from Smithville University and a bachelor's degree in English literature from Smithville College.

President Arnie Smith also announced that Joe Jones has been promoted to chief financial officer, starting January 1. Jones has been Smithville Consulting business manager for the last seven years and has implemented many measures to improve profitability and financial accountability. Before joining the firm, he was senior accountant at Smithville Industries. Jones holds a bachelor's degree in art history from the University of Smithville.

TEMPLATE

NEWS RELEASE
SMITHVILLE CONSULTING

Date of Release Goes Here

Contact: Person's name, phone number (with area code), and email address

Headline should focus on the position and person named to it

The first paragraph should showcase the big news—the hiring, promotion, or accomplishments at your company. It should identify the person by their most widely known accomplishment (book author, leader at another organization, longtime industry veteran) and note the effective date of their promotion or hiring.

"The quote should welcome a new hire to the organization, or call attention to what the person being promoted has achieved," said Person Making Announcement, Job Title. "If someone is retiring or departing for other reasons, thank them for their service and wish them all the best."

The third paragraph should provide a concise biography of the person—their most recent position, highlights of their career, noted accomplishments, and education. Other paragraphs for other people mentioned in the story—people who are retiring or being promoted—should follow the same pattern as this paragraph.

NEWS RELEASE—CALENDAR ITEM

Calendar items are shorter versions of advance stories. They're designed to promote an event over a period of time by being included in a media outlet's calendar of events. Each publication will have a different style, but this general format will work with slight modifications for most opportunities.

SAMPLE

NEWS RELEASE—CALENDAR ENTRY
SMITHVILLE GARDEN CLUB

October 24, 2021

Contact: Person's name, phone number (with area code), and email address

Smithville Garden Club to hold annual Greenhouse Open House on April 10

Greenhouse Open House, April 10, 10 a.m.–4 p.m., Smithville Garden Club, 500 Smithville Road, Smithville. New greenhouse tour, presentations on gardening, taste tests of fresh produce. Advance registration is not required. Proof of COVID-19 vaccination or recent test required at the door. 555-555-5555 or greenhouse@smithvillegardenclubwebsite.com.

TEMPLATE

NEWS RELEASE—CALENDAR ENTRY
SMITHVILLE GARDEN CLUB

Date of Release Goes Here

Contact: Person's name, phone number (with area code), and email address

Headline here has basic information, including date

Name of Event Here, date, times open, sponsor, address/location. Brief over-
view of activities, noted speakers, attractions—the "why" people will want to attend. Mention whether registration is required and if so how people should register. Mention details on COVID-19 policy. End with phone number and email
address for people with questions to contact.

NEWS RELEASE—CRISIS HOLDING STATEMENT

A holding statement is your first line of defense in crisis communications. It's a relatively short item designed to provide preliminary but verified information to the media, giving your organization some breathing room while you figure out what to do and say next.

A good holding statement should offer basic facts that can be confirmed with the officials in charge, such as a very vague description of the situation. It should not speculate or go further than what the incident commander is willing to say at this point in time. You don't want bad information to be out in the world.

It should also express empathy for those involved and project a feeling of comfort and calm to the reader. Those last two items are the most difficult to write but the most important.

The example below is not a conventional news release, but a statement issued in the name of an organization's leader. When you don't have all the facts to tell a complete story, then that format has its definite advantages—you don't need all the details at this point. Say what you need to say and move on.

SAMPLE

NEWS RELEASE
SMITHVILLE HIGH SCHOOL

October 24, 2021

Contact: Person's name, phone number (with area code), and email address

Smithville High School issues statement on bomb threat

Smithville High School Principal Sherry Smith issued the following statement today:

Smithville High School has been placed on lockdown and is being secured by the Smithville Police Department after a bomb threat was received this morning. I want to reassure parents and guardians that your children are safe. The safety and security of our students and staff is our highest priority, and we take all such threats extremely seriously. Our staff trains and prepares for incidents of all types with regular drills and tests. Parents should not come to the school to pick students up; we will inform parents directly via an automated call when the campus is fully secured and students may leave. We will share additional information as it becomes available.

TEMPLATE

NEWS RELEASE
SMITHVILLE HIGH SCHOOL

Date of Release Goes Here

Contact: Person's name, phone number (with area code), and email address

Headline is straightforward with who is saying it and why

Organization's name Leader's name issued the following statement today:

The first sentence should convey the basic facts of the case and the context that makes it important. The second sentence should express empathy and reassure participants or stakeholders. The third or fourth sentences should provide any important background of details that don't directly relate to the lead. The fifth sentence should include contact information and other loose-end details. The final sentence should state your commitment to sharing more information; if possible, try to let the media know an exact time when the next update will be coming out.

RECOMMENDED READING

No single book or website can capture everything that you need to know about public relations. A good PR person is always studying, reading, asking questions, and learning how to improve and level up their work.

I've read, consulted, and enjoyed a wide range of books that have helped my career get started and grow. Here are a few of the best.

The Word: An Associated Press Guide to Good News Writing, by René J. Cappon. This slender and unassuming book taught me the essentials of how to write a good news story—and turn a good one into a great one. It's not just a boring how-to-write book; there are countless examples throughout that would benefit any PR practitioner. Though it's now out of print, I strongly recommend picking up a used copy to add to your working library. If you can't find one, pick up *Writing the News*, by Walter Fox.

Creative Interviewing, by Ken Metzler. Another out-of-print book, this is a classic work written for journalists but which will help you prepare for any interview. It's a highly practical, hands-on treasure trove showing how to develop and ask the right questions—information that's essential to helping interviewees get ready to answer them.

Writing Without Teachers, by Peter Elbow. If you don't think of yourself as a writer, if you lack confidence in your skills, or if you hit writer's block whenever you sit down to bang something out, you need this book. A retired English professor, Elbow helped create a writing practice known as freewriting, which I mentioned in Chapter 4. His book is an excellent guide to breaking through barriers and getting words on the page.

Why School Communication Matters, by Kitty Porterfield and Meg Carnes. For those of us working in education, especially K–12 schools, this book is a lifesaver. I came to work for a countywide vocational-technical school district with no background in the special issues that arise in education, from complaining parents to criminal offenses. Porterfield and Carnes provide plenty of excellent examples and scenarios that can bring a new PR staff member up to speed—or help explain the need for good PR to a senior administrator.

Essentials of Thought Leadership & Content Marketing, by Paul M. Kaplan. This book is a great, practical handbook exploring in depth the items that I touch on in Chapter 9. Kaplan, who's been a marketer at American Express, McGraw Hill, and Princeton Review-Tutor.com, packs his book with details on audience research, content planning, generating leads, and calculating return on investment, among a host of other topics.

Building a StoryBrand, by Donald Miller. While this book is explicitly about marketing and brand development, the questions it poses are as important for a public-relations effort as they are for an advertising campaign. Miller's system helps you create better stories, think about the audience's place in them, and develop ideas for new content that can attract people. It's a valuable resource for any storyteller.

Contagious, by Jonah Berger. Penned by a Wharton School marketing professor, this book showcases research and case studies to introduce and explain the common elements that help products, campaigns, and companies rise in popularity. It has great insights for communications experts, especially the chapter on stories—it's worth the price of a paperback by itself.

The Associated Press Stylebook. Most media outlets in the US use AP style, developed by the Associated Press news organization to streamline all the tiny details that can hurt readers' comprehension and understanding. The *Stylebook* contains all those rules, with entries on using numbers, capitalization of job titles, how to abbreviate states, the proper terminology for technology, business, sports, and much more. I don't recommend actually sitting down and reading it cover to cover, because it's a fairly dense encyclopedia—but having it on hand as a reference work and consulting it frequently is a good idea. The more your news release matches AP style, the less editing someone is going to have to do.

Your local newspaper. If you're trying to get media attention and you're not reading your targets on a weekly or daily basis, then you're missing out. Pick up a copy—or better yet, subscribe—and read the articles regularly. You'll develop better writing skills and a greater understanding of how to frame an article.

WORKS CITED

Chapter 1: PR Isn't Hard

A certain degree of trust: "State of Public Trust in Local
News," 2019, by the Knight Foundation's Trust, Media and
Democracy initiative, https://knightfoundation.org/reports/
state-of-public-trust-in-local-news/.

Chapter 4: Write It So They'll Run It

The power of headlines: "How Headlines Change the Way We
Think," 2014, by Maria Konnikova, newyorker.com/science/
maria-konnikova/headlines-change-way-think.

Chapter 5: The Media

Researching the media: "Vanishing Newspapers," 2020, by Penelope
Muse Abernathy, Knight Chair in Journalism and Digital
Media Economics, Hussman School of Journalism and Media,
University of North Carolina, usnewsdeserts.com/reports/
news-deserts-and-ghost-newspapers-will-local-news-survive/
the-news-landscape-in-2020-transformed-and-diminished/
vanishing-newspapers/.

"More Than 90 Local Newsrooms Closed During the Coronavirus
Pandemic," 2021, by Kristen Hare, Poynter Institute, poynter.
org/locally/2021/the-coronavirus-has-closed-more-than-60
-local-newsrooms-across-america-and-counting/.

"Newspapers Fact Sheet," 2021, Pew Research Center, pewresearch.
org/journalism/fact-sheet/newspapers/.

"Research: More Stations Produced More Local News Than
Ever during 2020," 2021, Radio Television Digital News
Association, rtdna.org/article/research_more_stations_
produced_more_local_news_than_ever_during_2020

Ad sales and the journalism wall "SPJ Code of Ethics," 2014, Society
of Professional Journalists, spj.org/ethicscode.asp.

Chapter 6: The Details

Tidy up your desk: "Seymour M. Hersh—the Journalist as Lone
Wolf," 2018, by Alan Rushbridger, nytimes.com/2018/06/13/
books/review/seymour-m-hersh-reporter.html.

Real stories from real people: "Man Featured at Giuliani Press
Conference Is a Convicted Sex Offender," 2020, by Matt
Friedman, politico.com/states/new-jersey/story/2020/11/09/
man-featured-at-giuliani-press-conference-is-a
-sex-offender-1335241.

Chapter 7: The Art of the Interview

Finding spokespeople: "Cracking the Code on Food Issues: Insights
from Moms, Millennials and Foodies," 2014, The Center for
Food Integrity, foodintegrity.org/wp-content/uploads/2015/08/
CFI2014ResearchBook.pdf.

Chapter 9: Curveballs and Crises

Don't panic: "Coping with Fatigue, Fear, and Panic During a Crisis,"
2020, by Tony Schwartz and Emily Pines, https://hbr.org/2020/03/
coping-with-fatigue-fear-and-panic-during-a-crisis.

INDEX

ACKNOWLEDGMENTS

This book would not have been possible without the contributions of many friends and colleagues from the public relations, marketing, and journalism worlds who contributed ideas or feedback throughout the writing. Some have no idea that they helped, but they did so just by being there to bounce ideas off of or providing inspiration.

For their contributions to the insights shared throughout these pages, I especially want to thank Brent Addleman, Greg Bassett, Bruce Bishop, Aaron Chusid, Chris Eccleston, Sarah Fenske, Karen Foster, Amy Higgins, Kim Hoey, Adam Horwitz, Chrissy Kadleck, Kathie Klarreich, Ben Nagy, Brian Selander, Greg Star, Rachel Swick Mavity, Jeremy Tucker, Matt Westerhold, and Justin Williams.

For being generally great friends, people, coworkers, teachers, and leaders, I need to thank Bobbi Albright, Angie Basiouny, Anas ben Addi, Kenny Bounds, John Brady, Dr. Anne Colwell, Susan Eliason, Patti Ewald, the late Dr. John Gates, Marlena Gibson, Dr. Nancy Grace, Dawn Grenier, Steve Guthrie, Chip Guy, Stacey Hofmann, Ed Kee, Dr. James Keegan, the late Tim Konski, Alison May, the late Molly Murray, John Petersen, Holly Porter, Patricia Rivera, John Sell, Austin Short, Kim Speicher, Julie Wallace, Mary Ann Warrington, Joe Weber, Chris Whaley, Deb Whidden, Lisa Wildermuth, Andrea Wojcik, and the late Dr. Bill Williams. For their guidance and wise counsel taking this book from idea to the printed page, I want to thank the team at Quill Driver Books, including Kent Sorsky, Mariah Bear, David Sweet, and the people at The Reading List. I never quite realized just how much writing a book is a team effort.

For their love and support, I want to thank my family, parents, and friends, without whom this would never have been possible. My kids, Dassi, Matty, and Liam, deserve a huge thanks for putting up with me during the months it took me to write this. They're each amazing in their own special way.

My wife, Rachel Kipp, needs her own page of thanks. She's the lead of my story.

ABOUT THE AUTHOR

 **Dan Shortridge** is a communications and marketing consultant with more than 20 years of experience in the trenches of local public relations and daily newspaper journalism. He's worked for state and local government agencies, leading PR and marketing for Delaware's housing and community development agency and the state's agriculture department, as well as helping support private businesses and regional nonprofit organizations. He also handled communications and marketing for a countywide vocational-technical school district.

Before entering public service, he worked for 11 years as a reporter, copy editor, and designer at local newspapers in Delaware, Maryland, and Ohio. A national award–winning reporter, he was part of a team that won a national Sigma Delta Chi Award for Public Service Journalism from the Society of Professional Journalists and was an Ochberg Fellow with the Dart Center for Journalism and Trauma.

Dan's articles on crisis communications, social media marketing, and recruitment marketing have been published in national business-to-business magazines and statewide business publications. He is the coauthor of three local-interest books about Delaware and Maryland's Eastern Shore. Dan holds a master's of education in instructional design and a bachelor's degree in business administration–marketing, both from Western Governors University.

He lives in Delaware with his wife, Rachel, and their children.

CPSIA information can be obtained
at www.ICGtesting.com
Printed in the USA
JSHW061524160922
30490JS00004B/6